The Book of Number

Client Psychology

The Science of Understanding the Client in Pythagorean Numerology

Book Three in the Book of Number Quartet

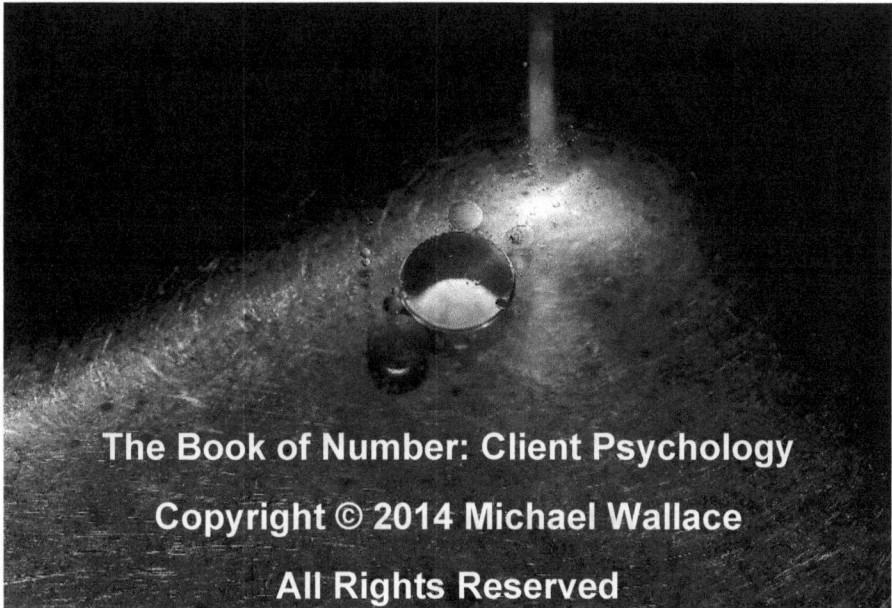

Published by Ladder to the Moon Publications.
ISBN: 978-0-9756994-5-4
Mail: PO Box 1355 Kingscliff, NSW 2487 Australia

The most momentous thing in human life is the art of winning the soul to good or evil.

Pythagoras

Other Books by the author:

Jerimiah Versus the Grabblesnatch

The Divinity Dice Series

Ratology: Way of the Un-Dammed

Hello Planet Earth

Welcome to the Book of Number: Client Psychology

This book is a study of the spiritual or "inner" view of the client that was originally presented preceding each chapter of the "Magic of Numbers" correspondence course. It was meant to assist the would-be practitioner in understanding their client, but also to help them grasp the nature of their OWN psychology.

Everything here is based in hard experience and years of observation. Client Psychology is common sense mixed with practical wisdom, as derived from the Pythagorean tradition, and the reader ideally will treat it as an "ancient" Self-Help manual.

You will find some terms that are in current use, such as "The Censor" (this comes out of Jungarian Psychiatry) but the views expressed are not aligned to the current teaching in that discipline. Similarly do we treat the concept of the ID in a rather alternative view.

Everything contained herein has been tested in real life situations over the course of many years. It may be considered too spiritual by some, or not practical enough by others, and academics will find the lack of annotation annoying. Be that as it may, what is here WORKS.

What matters is this: The author has a close to 100% success rate in identifying the core issues driving his clients. This is simply because the principles and ideas expressed herein were understood and followed. It must be noted, people come to see a Numerologist for many and varied reasons, but at heart, most wish the following:

- To alter a present condition, be it health, financial or otherwise

- To have a relationship work, or to create a relationship

- To understand themselves, or their partner, better

People rarely come to a Numerologist to solve mental or emotional conditions they are suffering with. If they do, best practice is to refer them to a specialist in the field where their concerns lay. That said, most people have some mild type of mental, emotional or stress condition, they are unaware of, that is triggering their real world concerns. So, while we must not pretend to be psychologists, this book will give you a grasp of the internal dynamics that drive people.

ORIGINAL "MAGIC OF NUMBERS" COURSE STRUCTURE

Understanding the Client: Psychology of Clients
Client Profiling: ID Quotient
Understanding the Primary Birth Number: Fadic Numbers

Understanding the Client: The Elements
Resolving Primary Numbers: Dominant and Composite Numbers

Understanding the Client: The Four Querent Types
First level of the Chart: Noumenal Flow Chart

Understanding the Client: The Survival Scale
Cycles: A brief Study of CYCLES

Understanding the Client: MEDIA
Studies of the Matrix: General introduction

Understanding the Client: The Censor
Understanding Number Weight: NOUMENAL WEIGHT
Studies of the Matrix: Lines in the Matrix

A study of the basic Laws: Laws and Principles
Studies of the Matrix: Trines in the Matrix
Interpretations of Lines in the Matrix: (Link from: Trines in the Matrix)

The purpose of Virtue: Knowledge is Not Virtue
Studies of the Matrix: ADVANCED: Patterns in the Matrix

A study of Spiritual Harmonics: HARMONICS
Studies of the Matrix: ADVANCED: The Overlay Matrix

Further Harmonic Studies: Numero Ordo Selectorum
Important Variations in the Matrix: DOUBLETS
Added Items of Note: Symbols. Letters and their Meanings.

A Study in the Psychology of Choice: Vases at the Portal
Closing Comments: Harmonic Principles

INDEX

May Apollo, the God of Song, guide you

This book is in two distinct stages. First, understanding the mind and internal process at work in the individual. Second, we look at the universal laws and principles that govern all of life.

Yet behind all the technical information, a pure and ancient energy is flowing. And it flows through each of us. The real secret to grasping Client Psychology is to be found in tuning in to this "oracle" if you will.

The true success in understanding this work is only to be found when YOU become the Oracle.

BROTHERHOOD

*A*bsolutely core to the Pythagorean tradition, and the reason why it lasted so long, was not the science or the discovery of new fields in Math, it was the simple, and deep bonds of friendship that united each of the main members of the school at Croton.

The two key criteria for promotion to a place of importance within the school were aptitude (you had to know your stuff) but also a sense of friendliness. If you weren't naturally friendly, you were never brought into the inner circle.

Ken Littlehawk, an old friend, an elder from the Mi'kmaq tribe, once spoke to me of brotherhood. *"It is not a thing, a place or a time, but an acceptance. It is seeing the man before you, and accepting him, as he accepts you. It is natural to have a brother, it is natural to trust. It Is a natural thing that so many have forgotten, and fallen into a world of delusion, alcohol, drugs and confusion. Acceptance simply means being present, and silencing the whispers inside. Just being present means we accept life, and then we realise, life was always our brother, our mother, our father, our sister and our lover."*

By report, Cylon the Croton, a member of that cities elite, was infuriated at not being accepted into the inner circle of the Pythagoreans. He led a revolt that burnt the school down. Now we cannot know for certain the reasons behind peoples action, but by the actions of Cylon we can presume he was not a particularly friendly soul.

Yet the brotherhood survives. There is the fabled story of Damon and Pythias, that speaks of the depth of trust and friendship shared by the Pythagoreans.

Around the 5th century BC, Pythias and his friend Damon, both followers of Pythagoras, traveled to Syracuse. Pythias was accused of plotting against the tyrant of Syracuse, Dionysius I. As punishment for this crime, Pythias was sentenced to death.

Accepting his sentence, Pythias asked to be allowed to return home one last time, to settle his affairs and bid his family farewell. Not wanting to be taken for a fool, the king refused, believing that once released, Pythias would flee and never return.

Damon offered to take his spot while he was gone. The king agreed, on the condition that, should Pythias not return when promised, Damon would be put to death in his place. Damon agreed, and Pythias was released.

Dionysius was convinced that Pythias would never return, and as the day Pythias promised to return came and went, Dionysius prepared to execute Damon. But just as the executioner was about to kill Damon, Pythias returned.

Apologizing to his friend for his delay, Pythias told of how pirates had captured his ship on the passage back to Syracuse and thrown him overboard. Dionysius listened to Pythias as he described how he swam to shore and made his way back to Syracuse as quickly as possible, arriving just in time to save his friend.

Dionysius was so pleased and astonished with their friendship that he pardoned them both. It was also said that Dionysius then sought to become their third friend, but was denied.

Many stories are said, but the experience of true brotherhood is something far beyond words. To stand with others, share their experience, and sit in joy of the present moment is something few people in Western Society understand. The closest common bond is now in the armed services. When you have faced adversary and death with another, you are forged together in a bind that cannot be broken, except by deceit.

In preparing for this book, on the night of a blood moon (partial lunar eclipse) I was taken out of the body, back to the time of the Pythagoreans. I witnessed how, on the day a solar eclipse occurred that the brotherhood was formed. Four men at the top of a mountain went to the point Pythagoras said would be the best place to witness this "miracle" of the Sun disappearing. And it did! So in awe, and so overwhelmed with the shared experience, the men were united in a way none could break. Pythagoras himself took on an almost god-like appearance to the fellows, because who else but a demi-God could know the movements of the stars and sun? This became the heart of the Pythagorean movement. In looking up the records and comparing this to the known approximate date of 530 BC for the forming of the famed Croton school, I noted that between 535 and 529 BC there were no less than 18 solar eclipses.

Given that Pythagoras' original teacher, Thales, is recognized as the first person to accurately predict a solar eclipse, it is likely he taught his student the math required to do so. And keep in mind, being able to predict such a matter means that Pythagoras must have understood the earth rotated the sun AND had sufficient and accurate measurements in place to predict it's movement. For the average person, this would be a matter of inestimable consequence. An eclipse in ancient times was seen as, literally, the shadow of the divine falling upon the earth. For the Moon and the Sun to disappear and reappear confirmed the ancient myths of death and resurrection. This was also core to the Pythagorean tradition. Reincarnation was an accepted truth.

I awoke from this experience, and a core question that had often made me wonder was answered. Why Croton? Yes, it is known that Pythagoras met and married a woman from Croton, but is this enough to uproot an entire teaching?

Why did the Pythagoreans go to Croton?

If I had a successful school in a capital city, lots of people knowing I was there, and people coming to see me, I really do not pack up and head to another city without a very good reason. Something motivated them to move and start a school in a far away land. There had to be some significant impulse, something that held a powerful conviction for them to settle in such an out of the way place.

Croton was no small city, and in 510 BC raised an army of 100,000 men to conquer a rival city. But it was not Syracuse, a cosmopolitan center for the arts. It was most known for its athletes, who regularly won the Pythian Games. We will never know the true reason why they moved, there is no authoritative reference. What is known is that the Pythagoreans were welcomed and esteemed in

that place. Now, I consider it a possibility that the series of eclipses in that period were seen as an omen of rebirth. Croton was literally the Pythagoreans re-birthing as a new creature.

Wherever the driving force to move, the underling brotherhood of the Pythagoreans and the central theme of friendship was at the heart of their existence. A person simply did not progress in the order if they were not part of this inner connection.

Sadly, this deep sense of connectedness to your tribe has all but vanished in modern society. People lock their doors, hide their children, and live in fear of strangers. Nothing could be further from the Pythagorean tradition.

History tells us the Pythagoreans moved and started a school at Croton. History also tells us that Pythagoras accepted women as well as men into his brotherhood of learning. History also tells us that the cream of Athenian youth, and indeed, many from all over Greece, came to learn at the foot of this ancient master. We may never know why it occurred, but we know it did. Curiously, amongst all the "firsts" listed above, the Pythagoreans were also the first society of registered communists. If you were a part of the inner circle, you gave everything you had to the order. However, should you choose to leave, this was given back to you, plus 10%. So it was a capitalist kind of communism! This really underpins the brotherhood concept. You needed nothing else but the brotherhood. You were an organic part of the whole.

We see this echoed in the modern day, where people are unified with an interest. A person who buys a classic Jaguar car, for instance, is really buying into a brotherhood of other like-minded souls, who will help you source parts, offer advice, and show you ways to care for the car. Any group unified with a common interest, ideally, will bring out the nature of brotherhood in both the person and the group.

So why do I mention this? Why is this the first chapter in a book on Client Psychology? The reason is very simple, because it is a core principle in the Pythagorean tradition. People with problems will usually suffer one thing more than anything else: Loneliness. Apart from the question they are asking, the deeper concern is generally one that comes about from the need for real friendship. Very few people have this. Without true, resonant friendship, we carry with us a sense of separation or isolation. This is so very often the root cause of the internal and external issues within our life.

What is a Friend?

A Brazilian man I met in passing once spoke to me about what was the most important thing in life. *"People in Western Culture like to think your job, or your money, or owning a good car are important. But if you have all of these things, and no friends, you are poor. If you are really poor, a friend will feed you, clothe you, look after you. A friend is your only real security in this life, your only true asset that you take with you past this life. A friend is the most important thing in the world."* So very true.

When I was a child I had no interest in other children until I went to school. There I saw people forming into groups, and I felt very alone. I knew I needed a friend, yet I had no idea how you created this. At age Four I was thinking, "What is a friend?" Let's face it, there's no manual you receive that explains how you make a friend, what a friend is, or how any of it works. It really puzzled me.

I can say that I felt I had only one true friend throughout most of my school years. It was no one's fault but my own, I didn't understand what a friend was.

At age 14, however, when at a new school and trying to make friends, I was with a group of kids and happened to comment about the big nose of some fellow we all knew. For some reason, I thought if I could get people to collectively laugh about another, then this would make me their friend. Stupid, isn't it, how we think? Right away a boy, who we will call Bob, turned around and said, *"What, your nose is perfect?"*

It hit me like lightning: Here was a true friend. Why? Because if Bob would defend a fellow he hardly knew, I realised I could TRUST him not to stab ME in the back. CLICK! The light went on: Trust. It was all about trust. Faithfulness, trustworthiness, honesty and integrity are core to the building of true friendship. And the driving force is a need.

The need is basic. I also realised that, while Bob was direct and clear, he was also being incredibly intimate. I mean intimate in the true sense of the word, which means there were no barriers between us. He stood, open, unafraid, and spoke his truth. If I didn't like it, tough. And if I wanted to argue, he was ready to stand his ground. For the first time in my life I felt truly connected to another human being.

A deep sense of relaxation flowed through me in a way that cannot be put into words. I discovered a true sense of intimacy because I could trust Bob to be himself. This was the astounding simplicity of it all. Many years later, when Bob confided to me his deepest, darkest secret, I was able to return that trust in a way that affirmed his way of living. Now, I haven't seen him for years, but I still FEEL this connection. It is with me always. This is brotherhood.

So right off the bat, I want you to know that core to this ENTIRE PROCESS is this sense of trust, and the subsequent sense of intimacy. If you can inspire your client in the same way Bob inspired me, if you can stand and simply speak your truth, you will succeed. If you introduce to your clients the core truths that are present in their chart, show them the things they came here to learn, and present this to them in an open, clear and absolutely courageous manner, you will succeed. More, you will become truly useful.

Trust, Confidence and Honesty are Core to a Numerical Reading

I am here to speak my truth. You are here to speak your truth. When you understand this book, you will be able to speak the truth your client is inwardly longing to hear.

And it is always something obvious, and simple. As an example: A woman came to me asking about a lost love, and asked if would he come back. My initial response was something she didn't expect. *"First: Are you worthy of being loved?"* I asked her.

"What?" she stammered, *"I just want to know if he will come back."*

"Is this what you came here for?" I am guessing she didn't usually go to readers who asked questions of her like this. *"Let me put it another way, you feel an empty space where a person you loved used to be, yes? (she nods) And what you really want is that empty space to be filled, so you don't feel this loss you suffer, yes? (she nods again) So tell me: Can you imagine a person, deep inside, who is so confident in herself, so sincerely strong and independent within her being, that she no longer NEEDS this person in order to feel whole?"*

She broke down in tears. *"Yes!"* she said. *"This is what I want."*

I had not even put pen to paper or worked a single thing out, yet the true purpose of the reading was already clear. Now it was just finding the path within her chart that would lead her to the strong, independent woman she always had wanted to be.

Curiously, at the end of an hour session, she asked, *"Will he come back to me?"*

"Do you still want him to?" I asked.

She looked into the distance and said, *"No, I don't need him anymore."*

Feeling a sense of brotherhood is what allows this sort of clarity to occur. When you are truly connected inside yourself, when you are truly connected with the flow of life in and around you, clarity occurs within your heart. In this state, it is easy to see where others are disconnected, and why they are unhappy. Learning to re-connect with the inner divine, this is the reason we are here. What we are doing with Number Analysis is a genuine and, in the real meaning of the word, a truly religious thing. Don't mistake the word "religion" for priests and dogma, that is something else.

The word religion itself comes from the Latin verb "Religare", to re-unite, or re-tie.

People come to see a Numerologist because something is broken. There is some sort of disconnect in their life that they want repaired. It may appear to be a question about their love life, or business interests, but underneath this there is always a deeper driving force, a deeper yearning. If you can identify this, bring it out into the open, you will be able to truly help your client.

What's more, you will also reveal yourself to *yourself* in a deeper and more intimate manner. This will allow you to create a deeper, stronger and clearer connection with your own life. That's the nature of true brotherhood: As we share our truth, we discover it. As we discover it, we share it. And in sharing it we are set free.

Welcome to the Book of Number: Client Psychology. I trust you will find the journey undertaken within these pages to be eventful, intriguing, and sustaining in the many months and years to come. Absorb these pages, soak in them, and allow them to open up inside you. At some point, you may see fit to enter into the ancient brotherhood, and become a practicing analyst that will help people live their lives better.

UNDERSTANDING THE CLIENT

*M*any consider this book on Client Psychology to contain the most significant and interesting information in the Book of Number series. Of course, the working out of the various Patterns and Aspects, then resolving these into their interpretations, is detailed and takes time to master, but in the end this is really fairly mechanical. The real secret is in communicating this information to the client in a way that connects and is understood.

This requires a solid grasp of human psychology. In this book we will look at understanding the client, or what we call the Querent. (The person asking the question or seeking an answer) Here we open up the inner workings of the human state and the various shades and aspects of the internal person. In simple terms: If we are to truly serve and understand the person we are doing a reading for, we must develop the ability to read THEM, not just their chart.

Please note that the Client Psychology Study is lined up in a specific order. Like the course proper, these sections are meant to be read in the order in which they appear.

In this way, we work with a "line of resonance" that will build upon itself to ensure you get the clearest possible understanding of what we are giving to you.

When writing the first Numerology Course in 1991, titled "The Magic of Number", I noticed clear and distinct synchronicity at work. So often found that when I needed to work on some particular Aspect,in the course I would get a string of charts that all had THAT particular Aspect highlighted. It happened time and time again, and I understood that this is all part of the Law of Resonance. Things like this are the reason for this book.

What is the Law of Resonance? We take up a study of the Laws in: Laws and Principles

This book is a fairly intense compilation of over 40 years experience. There is much to learn and come to grips with in this area of number reading, and it may take years before it really connects. Suffice to say, every single chapter in the following pages has been verified by the many thousands of clients who have come through my door.

One thing I promise you, if you truly come to grasp the meaning and intent of this book on Client Psychology, you will never need a psychiatrist to help you solve life's issues. At its core, this is a book on how to be truly self-sufficient, confident and aware. It is a book of self-revelation, as much as it will help you to understand others.

If you desire to know more about the type of natural philosophy you find in these pages please buy my book, "Ratology: Way of the Un-Dammed". (Available on Amazon)

ID Quotient

This is a pun on IQ. Everyone is so fussed on the IQ, how smart someone is, but IQ never solved personal issues. What really counts is the state of self-worth, which is aligned with the degree you "own" your sense of Identity. Thus: Your Quota of Identity

It is essential when compiling an accurate chart to "read" the person as much as you read the chart. This is not the clothes they wear or how they act, but the little things: the way they hold their shoulders, the way they look at something in the room. All this will tell you where they are at on the Survival Scale, and where their attitude is. This directly affects their personal sense of Identity. How you see them is one thing, how they see themselves is another. The job is to understand how they see themselves!

It is the IDENTITY Quotient we are looking for here, not IQ, nor the Social graces.

This is the area of esteem, and strongly relates to a person's ability to interact with others in a way that enhances or disavows their expression of individuality.

How do you get a feel for the level of self-identity a person has? It is really very simple. Firstly, we need to realize there are two types of Identity. First, the false states of self-belief that are delusional, and second, the natural levels of self-belief, which are the core truth for the individual. The second is the childlike state. Those in this state are generally quite accepting of others. The other is a manufactured state, and this person invariably is concerned about how they appear and what others think of them.

As a simple example. Anyone wearing a ton of makeup, or particularly gaudy clothes, or mis-matched colors, or anyone who is louder than they need be: These folk tend to be working on expressing a false self-image. Not always, but generally this is the case.

People who come in with genuine smiles, and who tend to be fairly bright of nature tend towards a more natural level of self-esteem. It really is often just this simple. **Look how children are, and how they relate. This will give you the best clue to how to pick false and genuine levels of Self-Esteem and Identity.**

Next, watch the behavior.

A person with a strong identity will listen to what you say, and respond to it in a way that feels right to them. A person, and this is the majority of people, with a low sense of self, a LOW Identity Quotient, will listen to what you say, but only through the filter of what they want to hear, or what they expect to hear. They really do not hear you.

These are the type that go to the psychic purely to get some advice on a trivial matter, and only pay attention only if the advice is sounding like what they want.

Another low ID type, one that has a fragile sense of esteem, will compare and match everything to patterns they have seen in the past. They will take any words you say, and invariably have some sort of story of their own that they believe matches what you are saying. Generally, it is a filling-in of empty space that the person is really doing, and as a rule, we just allow this to occur. Perhaps in time the real message will get through.

Often we are in the situation where we cannot say what we really feel. Perhaps this is because you sense that it will not really be clear to the person, or won't connect with this individual. Invariably this is because of the level of Self-Esteem you, or they, are at.

However, nothing is perfect and it is not our job to be 100% right. The job is to interpret and communicate the number patterns as best we can. However, be aware that when people have low self-esteem and identity issues, it is very hard to gain any headway against the compressed problems and concerns that are really running their lives.

You simply won't make much of a difference with people who have little sense of themselves and little sense of self-worth.

We try and do what we can. However, it pays to note that people who have a healthy sense of themselves tend towards living a life-wish, and already carry an attitude of *"what do I have to do to move beyond the present situation"*. These folk want advice and confirmation and are no trouble at all. The reading tends to flow fairly easily.

People with a low sense of Identity tend towards a death-wish. They are not suicidal, so much as they tend to want to alter or change elements within the present situation to suit themselves. Where they ARE is never good enough. Everything you say will be interpreted in a way that fits the preset agenda that they have in their hearts. In other words: People with low self-esteem will hear what they want to hear. We need to just accept that this is the way it is, and allow them the freedom to walk their own journey.

Strong ID people tend to regard the needs of others. Low ID people tend to think the world owes them a favor. Naturally, you rarely, if ever, really meet someone who is totally clear in their identity, or totally lost and without identity.

Intelligence tends to rise with people who have a good sense of who they are, and this often makes the person easier to talk to, but this can also lift up their levels of vanity and arrogance, thus making it harder to relate to them.

It is all a juggling act of communication. Yet, it is made easier if we remember one thing.

At all times, remember that a person's sense of Identity is generally quite fragile. The best way to communicate is to avoid absolute statements. Some hints! Avoid the word "You" in any area that seem difficult. *"You may have an issue with ..."* is a poor phrase if you wish to communicate. Say, "*This pattern generally indicates this issue ...*" or perhaps "*Potentially this aspect leads to these options ...*" or similar words to that effect.

Use a third-person reference "*I knew a person with this pattern, and they experienced this effect*". You want to involve people in a dialogue, and not set up barriers inside them. Avoid a monologue, ask questions, and use inclusive language where possible.

There is also the type that have a strong, positive personality on the surface, but it can just collapse, and turn into a completely negative one. They are the Manic Depressive (bi-polar) types, and there are many more of them than we might suspect. Take care. I have seen people undergo a personality change during a reading, and this is LARGE warning sign. It is a clear indicator that the person has little sense of who they really are. It is also a sign to step back, and check if they are getting professional help. We are not their doctor.

I stress this once more: *Never seek to be a psychiatrist, or solve the issues that come from madness.* Step back. At times like this, you need to reserve the right to terminate a reading or chart compilation. Encourage people to see a doctor that specializes in the area of their problem.

Intention, not Hope!

It is a truism that we get what we expect, rather than what we wish for. This is the basis for the old Tibetan saying: "*Intention, not hope!*" Most people who come to you with a concern to solve, really have an intention problem. They have no clear direction, and are just hoping for the best. Your sense of Identity is really like a rudder on a ship. It steers us away from hope, and towards what we expect in life. Low ID = No Direction.

A strong ID can be equally troublesome, because of the vanity aspect that can arise with it, but it is easier to work with in the long term. So this all begs the question: *How do we enhance and encourage a strong, natural sense of Identity within our clients?* The very best way is for you to know yourself. Gnoeth Sueton. It is that simple.

If YOU have a strong sense of who you are, this will rub off onto your clients, and you will find people coming to you for this very reason. They may have some sort of external question, but inwardly they feel your certainty. This happens because of a simple principle, the Law of Resonance. (We cover these Laws in the Laws and Principles Section)

Never underestimate the power within the Law of Resonance. When you have a strong, independent sense of who and what you are, then people will come to you and listen. In truth, they will come to you to pick up this energy that they need and want, and the number reading of itself is really the sideshow.

(There was a point where I had to stop my public readings, because the following was getting a little out of hand. A little like the people pursuing Brian in Monty Pythons "Life of Brian", the flocks of people became intrusive. I moved to a country address, and started the correspondence course to stay in touch.)

The point is that when we have a strong sense of Identity, we move with INTENTION, not hope. Perhaps you feel you are worthless and are trying to find a sense of yourself through this study? It is still all good. Often it is BECAUSE we have a poor sense of Identity that we go looking for some purpose to help bolster it up. We can still be useful, even with all our frailties and problems. The truth is that the study of Number, and going through the difficult job of learning to master the variations and the techniques, will bring us to the point of having a better sense of who and what we are.

It's all a circle, and there is no good or bad relative to the wheel of life. We are all right where we are meant to be, but more, we can all change the set of the sail, and move in a different direction. It is the ID Quotient that gives you the WILL to re-set the sail.

Always remember, what you are seeing in a clients chart often has a meaning and purpose beyond what is apparent. Often the interaction of reader and client carries a two-fold purpose: Helping the client, yet also revealing something inside ourselves that needs resolving. In other words, by helping others, we grow within ourselves.

Our sense of worth, our sense of IDENTITY, is the starting point in any reading. When people sense that a person before them is secure in their own skin, the simple experience of this is often worth the cost of the reading for a person.

Remember, all is a frequency. We ARE the song of Life. Each Soul is a symphony.

Next we study the first of the spiritual aspects of the Inner Being: The Elements

Understanding the Client

The Elements

We all know of the basic elements, Earth, Wind, Fire and Water. We generally have some idea of the meaning of Fire, Water, etc. and how they relate to us via our astrological sign, etc. A Fire sign is lively, a Water sign contemplative.

Most now accept that the Fifth Element, that of Spirit, is also a powerful aspect worthy of consideration. All five aspects are continually cycling through our consciousness, combining and recombining in a myriad of patterns through every tick of the clock.

All these elements are at work in the basic psyche and physical makeup of every person, in every situation, and every potential circumstance. Recognizing the elemental forces at work within a person is one thing, knowing what it means is another, and so in this short section we will attempt to help you come to grips with this area of consciousness.

Few people understand the elements are at work within us every moment of the day, interacting, changing, forming new elements. Nothing is static, nothing is fixed, and everything is subject to change.

We have a PRIORITY element at work as a rule. For example: A person may have a lot of fire aspected in their makeup, or a lot of water. But there will constantly be other elements interacting and reacting to form new states in accordance with how the individual meets the changing circumstance of their day to day existence.

One way of seeing this is through the eyes of the natural world. It is axiomatic that truth exists in all planes, so if something is true in one area, it tends to lead us to a greater truth in another. So let's look at how the elemental forces work in the physical.

Fire (sun) meets earth and water, and wood is formed. The natural growth of forest requires all three to be able to exist. Fire from the Sun, nutrient from the Earth, and Water are necessary for a tree to grow. Yet is also needs Air, for the tree must breath.

Yet, obviously, Fire, Earth, Wind and Water combine in many other forms. Every living thing contains these four elements, but very few people have grasped what this cycle of creation is within the body. In this study we look at some arcane wisdom, and how the Pythagoreans viewed the "dance of elements".

Elements interact to create form, and are also eternally shifting in themselves. Fire can be a forest fire, a camp fire or a kiln, or even a star. Water can be rain, snow, ice, fluid, solid. Wind can be still or a gale, while earth can be soft or hard.

Soft Earth can grow flora, while a rock cannot. Water is necessary for life, but when it is too cold, it kills. Fire can cook the meal, or burn down the house.

Fire opposes water, earth opposes air. Air feeds fire, water feeds earth. Air has no relation to earth, but poorly oxygenated earth does not grow things very well. Earth needs fire from the sun to be able to sustain life, fire needs the air to burn.

The elements shift their quality and state (water becomes steam, etc.) in accordance with the strength and potency of the energy field they encounter. (And there are many energy signatures or energy fields that use the elements as catalysts)

There are Four Singular Elements:

FIRE	1	ORIGIN
AIR	2	DUALITY
WATER	3	CREATION
EARTH	4	GROWTH - DECAY

There are SIX combinations of 2 Elements:

FIRE - AIR	5	PASSIONATE, RESTLESS
FIRE - WATER	6	ACTIVE, PROGRESSIVE
FIRE - WATER	7	INTENSE, SPIRITUAL
EARTH - WATER	8	CALMING, RESOLUTE
WATER - AIR	9	DREAMLIKE, QUIESCENT
EARTH - AIR	10	DETACHED, CONTEMPLATIVE

There are FOUR Combinations of 3 Elements:

EARTH - AIR - WATER	11	PROGRESSIVE
FIRE - EARTH - AIR	12	INSPIRATIONAL
FIRE - WATER - AIR	13	INTUITIVE
EARTH - WATER - AIR	14	CONTENT

And just ONE combination of all Four Elements:

FIRE - EARTH - WATER - AIR   15   VARIABLE, COMPLETE

Once we accept that the physical cycle of elements is at work in the backdrop of life here on Earth, we can start to accept that this is also happening on a spiritual level.

In all, there are ELEVEN combinations of the Four Elements, plus the four "pure" or singular Elements. There is a clear correlation between the Element Combinations and Number, seen above and on the previous page. NB: This "elemental cycle" relates to the "Magic Square" principle, where every line in a nine box magic square adds to 15. This is too in-depth to cover in a book. We will have info at bookofnumber.com.au.

Look at a client as they walk in, and see if you can begin to pick what type they are. Keep in mind that while a person has a basic "metabolism', every day, hour and minute we are shifting shift into some other elemental combination. This is as a natural result of the cycles that are active in our lives.

Overall, as you develop a feel for it, when a person walks through the door you will have a sense of the elements at work in that moment. Very often, if they are a Seven Birth Number, they will vibrate to Fire - Water. It is not fixed, but relatively common.

Be aware that ALL the above elemental types exist within every person. And they modulate between an active and a passive mode, as well as a positive and a negative polarity. This we take up in the next section of Client Psychology, the Four Querent Modes.

For the present, if someone appears dreamlike and focused on some other world when you see them, then it is likely they are going through the "Water - Air" combination. This is only for the present moment and at any stage their next cycle can start, which is possibly Earth-Air (10) or whatever is a likely cycle in the person's chart.

And here is the big secret. A person will move along the elemental table in exact accordance with the pattern of number present in their chart

In other words, a quiet dreamy person can change overnight, and become whatever it is that is scheduled for the next tick of their inner psychic/spiritual clock. What is more, the patterns of number in their chart will indicate the pattern of progression through their elemental types. If a 1-5-9 Line of Success is strong, they will likely cycle from Fire, Fire - Water, Water - Air in their attitude when striving for success, as an example.

As a note, a person with a lot of fire will generally be more comfortable near water. A person with a lot of water will be more comfortable high up, nearer the air. A person with a lot of air will be happier in a country home. Mostly, the opposite to what people are is where they find greatest happiness, with the exception that a person with a lot of earth will love to have solid earth-like things around them. They love travel, however.

Mostly we find "earth" types have a desire for Earth, both practically and metaphysically. (I know it sounds a pun, but it isn't) The tendency here is for solidarity, firm foundations, safety in numbers, that sort of thing. Yet secretly the Earth types are all dreaming of romance and fire! Earth types often bring ruin on their families and personal lives when they fall in love with a mistress, etc.

The Fire type loves to create, to find new horizons. They literally burn to discover the new. The Air type tend to be dreamers, easily swayed by the prevailing breeze, or they ARE the prevailing breeze. The Water type are literally fluid, unless they have been locked in place by their upbringing. Then they are like ice, cold and rigid. It is all a little self-explanatory when you grasp the general idea.

The Elements are connected to the Querent Types (following chapter), which is another study that is important, and these two combine to form the essential characteristics we need to know about a person when they come for a reading.

One of the basic reasons to grasp some sort of understanding about Elemental types is to help identify how best to communicate with a person. There is absolutely no use trying to use flowery language with a fire type, for instance. They like things clear, condensed and to the point. Whereas a water person would find this repulsive, and would read that you are trying to control them.

There is no clear guideline, other than you work this out as you go along. Your OWN elemental nature will call for a specific type of practice in dealing with others, but safe to say, what we are seeking to obtain is the "combined state" where all is bound by spiritual essence. You will know when you achieve this. All things become transparent.

As a summary:

Fire-based personas need focus and clarity. No beating around the bush, tell them the facts, and give them a clear idea of direction.

Water-based people need empty space and silence between the words you speak. They need to soak in the vibration, and are often very intuitive. Questions, like "Does this feel right to you?" or "Do you have a sense that confirms this?" work best.

Earth-based people love mystery, and seeing someone in a weird head dress in a tent saying cryptic things about life is absolutely wonderful for them. You can abuse them, shout at them, and it is all water under the bridge, as long as you are interesting,

Air-based people love broad, sweeping statements. Quoting lines from ancient texts is seen as a thing of beauty, and a sense of being unhurried yet detailed is very important to them. They LOVE details.

No single person is all just one Element, but in this you will recognize a general spectrum of the type of people you will meet.

The next aspect of Understanding the Client comes with another group of Four: The Four Querent Types.

The Four Querent Types

We have already looked at the Elements at work in everyone's nature, and now we take a close look at the basic modes of expression, known as the **Four Querent Types**. This concept you will not find noted anywhere else other than it's analogy in ancient Egyptian Texts. (The Compass Points)

In essence, the idea is simple. People are moving between poles of Active or Passive, as well as Positive or Negative, in their outlook and expression. A QUERENT is a person seeking answers to questions. All people that come to ask you a question about themselves or a situation they face will fall into one of the following categories.

The Four Querent Types are defined as follows:

1. **Active - Positive (Assertive, Directed)**

2. **Active - Negative (Controlling, Manipulating)**

3. **Passive - Positive (Calm, Contemplative)**

4. **Passive - Negative (Social, Insecure)**

The above States are MUTABLE, or subject to change. A person can come in to a room being the very assertive "Active-Positive" type but in the space of a few minutes they can revert to Active-Negative, or flip to Passive Positive. People are NOT fixed to any one type for an entire lifetime. In fact, people will change the "presentation" of their Querent Type from moment to moment.

The way this works is denoted in Psychology Journals under various concepts such as "Passive Aggressive" converting to "Dominator" etc.

As an example: A father may be Active - Positive to his children, but virtually reverse and become Passive - Negative when dealing with an overbearing wife. This is usually based in him having a lack in confidence. More importantly, we need to remember that this is not the exception to the rule, but the norm. People flip and flop between many internal poles on a continual basis, depending on outer circumstance.

Even so: At the core of things, a person will have a priority signature that will be one (or more) of these four modes or types. It is common to see a person who is one "type" at home, and another "type" at work, for instance. It may sound like most people are two faced, but what is really happening is INSIDE the person is more like shifting gears to adapt to the changing circumstances. Even so, when you ask targeted and specific questions, you will see people revert back to their most basic "type".

Without going into too much at this point, this is one of the reasons a Numerologist keeps ASKING QUESTIONS of their clients. It not only QUALIFIES where you are at with a client, it keeps them from changing "type" too much.

We will not go into it here, but occasionally we meet someone who has integrated all four modes. This rare type is the personification of the poem, Desiderata. They rarely turn up for a reading, but if they do, you will be the one learning from them. You will see this "balanced aspect" in inquisitive children.

Spirit is like Breath - A Spiritual Exercise

Let's take a look at the OVERVIEW of what causes a TYPE to begin with. What we are talking about are the four basic ways people interact with the energy of Spirit as it enters their world. It is like spiritual breathing, and in truth, Spirit constantly flows in and out of our being. We can work with this!

A basic exercise given by the Paramahansa Yogananda (One of the few genuine masters to grace our planet in recent times) is a very powerful and very worthwhile thing to practice. You might like to stop and practice it for a moment. It is very simple.

Imagine you are breathing out as you breath in, and imagine you are breathing in while breathing out. Can you do this? It is a very effective exercise. If you do this for six weeks whenever you think of it, maybe 20 or more times a day, you will find your relationship with Spirit will be STRONGLY accented, and you will start seeing the world in a very different light. It is such a simple, and yet an extremely powerful exercise.

The Four Querent Modes are like a form of breathing.

It is not quite like breathing "in and out". The Passive mode is like holding your breath, the Active mode is like forced breathing. We obviously need a mix of the two.

If there is a goal in this study, it is to find a balance with the Negative and Positive energies within. The best picture we can hold is that of little children. They remain flexible with the tide of events, and ALLOW thing to happen around them. Conversely, the adult tends to try and DIRECT things. The Negative aspect tries to control, while the Positive aspect wants to be free. The Active wants to create change, the Passive wants to avoid it. All of us are pulled to some degree between these four poles, and most people sit somewhere in the middle of these four tensions, feeling vaguely stressed.

When we learn to relax into our natural self, the act of breathing the present moment in and out becomes a normal, natural state. The point of balance is found in the place where we find our natural self. Understanding this removes stress.

The ideal is a balanced inflow and outflow. The positive and negative energies will work together quite harmoniously, yet clearly in many peoples lives this is hardly the case. And remember, there is also Active and Passive to consider as well! Ideally we assist the client to find a balance in whatever their natural state might be.

The principle behind the Four Querent Modes is: NOTHING IS STATIC. All moves to a specific, and variable, dynamic.

It is, in truth, the RESONANCE generated between the four poles of Positive/Negative and Active/Passive that generates a powerful pulse and rhythm in our lives.

These energies are like magnets that pull and push our conscious thought, and create a good part of the patterns of life we experience. It is also a fact that a powerful person with a strong thought field can easily influence anyone who is unaware of this subtle interplay of energy. Our job is to help make people more aware, thus less controllable.

External Energies Affect Us (Invisible Control Strings)

The Positive/Negative and Active/Passive energies are like "strings" pulling at us from between the compass points. As someone seeks to move North to the Positive, they are tugging on the strings that attach them to the Negative, as well as the Active / Passive poles of their nature. We feel this in our lives as a tension of some sort.

It is like everyone lives in a cobweb. It is quite a trick to avoid the "Energy Strings" that rule each individual. But then we find there are also EXTERNAL "strings" controlling people. The EXTERNAL controllers, such as "guilt" and "shame" (to name but a few of the negatives) tie into these internal strings. And seek control an individuals thoughts.

It is like we are all puppets on a set of strings. What about free will, you ask? Social pressure and familial programming determines how most people will act, not free will. Of course, we need these things to keep order in society, but they are fences that keep you in, spiritually as well as physically. To be yourself, you have to break through the invisible threads that hold you in place.

I saw this many years ago. There was a time when I would look at a client and see filaments of light connecting them to their past, their fears, their programming. It was a little like they were puppets on a string, controlled by invisible forces. During this time, my 5 year-old son drew a perfect picture, a grumpy puppet tied to a set of strings. (Pictured)

I love this drawing. It says so much about the human condition! It takes a great deal for someone to snip through all the attachments and strings that tie us to our circumstances. If you are to serve any useful person, helping one person see how important it is to stand on your own two feet will make your time here on Earth a thing of value.

Becoming our own person, however, cutting the strings that tie and learning to dance around the control measures and guilt traps of socialized thought is quite a task. In African tribes, it is called "dancing the witch dance". There is a way to dance through the traps and projected energy that people seek to confine us with. It is a difficult task, but if we persist it leads us to the state where, as Thoreau stated, we become "a majority of one against the crowd".

THE FOUR QUERENT MODES: (Descriptions)

The basic energy sets that inhabit the human consciousness, and which we all share, are given in the interpretations after this chapter. Here we discuss a little of the mechanics, or energies that drive these aspects within us. These forces create "fields" of energy.

The fields are like (if you could see them on the Inner Planes) spiral patterns of energy that wind in and out of the consciousness. In the positive mode, the energy is expanding, in the negative, it is contracting. In the Active Mode the energy externalizes, in the Passive mode the energy internalizes. It is really that simple. You can see why I describe them as a sort of breath.

Energy moves in a spiral, and yet if we imagine we are looking at a clock, from front side of the face the arms are turning clockwise, but if we are INSIDE the clock, effectively looking behind the arms that move, it appears to be spinning anti-clockwise.

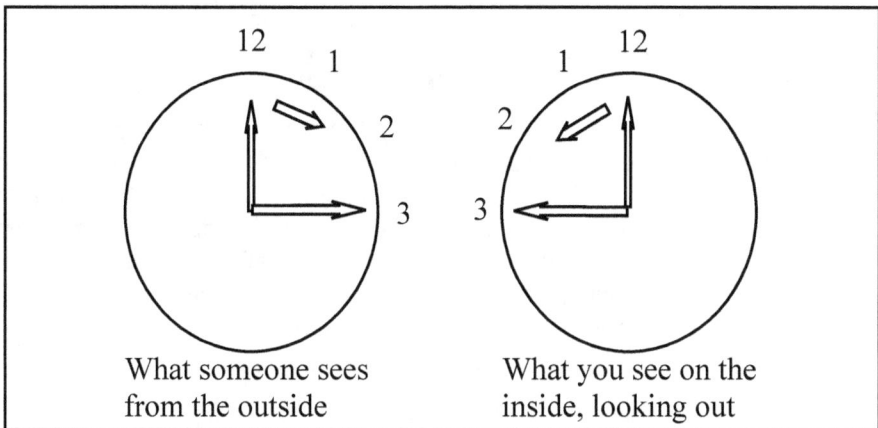

What someone sees from the outside   What you see on the inside, looking out

Have you ever felt that someone sees you as the opposite of what you are? Remember the "Clock Example" and it may help you to understand their viewpoint. A person who feels they are one thing, is often perceived as the opposite by those with a different mindset or viewpoint than the individual might hold. In a nutshell, this is why people choose certain religions and groups. Being with people who hold a similar view to their own makes life easier and less complicated. They are all "on the inside" so to speak.

HOWEVER: Here's the real Secret to it all. Even though it appears to the person on the "other" side of the clock that the energy is running in the opposite direction to how you perceive it, the **Order of the Number** remains constant. It is a basic truth: **The Order of Number never changes, regardless of the viewpoint we choose to take.**

Positive or Negative? Both are just ways of seeing things. They are simply "A" viewpoint, rather than anything like "The" right or wrong view. Pardon the terrible clock pun, but given time it will always change. All things will change, given enough time. It is only when we find the **neutral state** that we get the eye of the storm.

As a side note, if a person holds doggedly to their view being correct, people around them will slowly come into an accord with this. This is the Principle of ENTRAINMENT. But it creates enemies, and they also find themselves in overt and direct opposition to others. This is the Law of Polarity, which we deal with in the <u>Laws and Principles.</u>

The cute thing about the clock example is that it gives us a perfect example of the fragility of communication. A person looking at the clock says "It's Three O'clock" but the person INSIDE the clock will say "That looks like Nine O'clock to me!" Remember: The NUMBERS, for and of themselves, never change. What changes is our view of them.

The Positive DRIVES the Negative, and Vice Versa.

The Natural Result of Positive Energy is to create a equal and opposite negative reaction. This is basic Newtonian physics.

A further interesting thing we can understand here is how the Positive CREATES and then DRIVES the Negative, and vice versa. It is like cogs in a machine. One spins in one direction and drives the one adjacent to it in an equal and opposite direction.

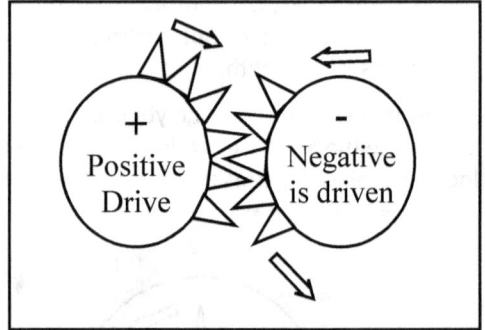

It is blindingly simple: If you did not engage the first cog, the other would not turn. By applying force of any sort, we create an equal and opposite reaction. In the same sense, like we have in the clock example, a person with a negative view of yourself can generate a significant reaction in you. Yet, if you do not engage that person's energy, there's no problem. This is the meaning of the Tibetan principle of being neither for nor against anything. It means external forces can no longer drive you.

Remember when I said how people tend to change their Querent type like the gears in a car, seeking to suit the circumstances they find themselves in? Well, here is where it applies in practice. People shift from one aspect to the other, trying to drive or control the causes and effects of life and situations around them.

The principle of gearing, that is, driving things faster or slower, is supplied with the EMOTIONAL energy of the individual. It is essentially changing the size of the cog that drives the other cog. This is NOT positive mental attitude. PMA tells you that when you become more and more positive, you will drive that negative feeling away! But the more power applied to the positive simply supplies more power to the negative. I tell clients to forget Positive Mental Attitude, and work with a Possibility Attitude.

An Ancient Greek maxim stated that given a sufficient leverage, you can move the world. Change the SIZE of the cog, and you slow down it's effect. By ENLARGING the sense of inner confidence, we change our relationship with the negative cog inside us. So develop that sense of "I am here now" and many issues fade away. In other words, rather than seeking to become more positive, focus on NOW, and feel this certainty.

Extending this to a Spiritual Principle, when the internal Positive and Negative gears in the human persona are properly engaged and working, the individual is then in a position to CHOOSE what gear they want to engage the external world with. Rather than churning in your own mind, you ENGAGE the world with the appropriate gear that will allow you to accomplish your task.

It is like driving a car. There's no good or bad, right or wrong gear. There is only the RIGHT gear for what is appropriate in the moment.

As a further extension: Using the negative gear, or approaching things in our life with a negative approach, tends to create a positive result in our external environment. A small negative gear can drive a much larger wheel.

It seems a paradox, but approaching things with a negative assessment can often solve many problems before they arise. Every good builder understands this principle. Look for the problems, look for the issues in the areas where things may go wrong, and you tend to get a clearer run with things when you get going.

Interpretations for the Four Querent Modes:

Think about this, if you will. So much of what we have been taught as "right" or "correct" is simply a viewpoint applied to your inner wheels, in order to make them turn in a way that is acceptable to society. When we stop accepting the "shoulds" and "should nots" of other people, we quickly discover that we are no longer driven by their options, nor are we controlled by our inner fears that gave them credence in the first place.

If we want to be free, we need to start with being aware.

What counts for the present is understanding the Four Basic Querent Types. At first it will seem an impossible task identifying the different types of people into the various modes, but as you learn to see the little signs, it becomes very clear.

So, in the following pages we give a detailed description of the type of effect generated by each of the Four Querent Modes.

In a broad description, the Positive/Active Life path is expansive and embracing of change. The Positive/Passive Life path tends towards poetic expression and other types of Introspection.

The Negative/Active Life Path indicates control and life negating attitudes while the Negative/Passive Life Path suggests a more robotic life existence.

As a small example, many people have never looked beyond the games of role playing in society, therefore they live more in the Negative/Passive mode. But at any time this person may fall in Love, and for a period convert to the Positive/Active life path.

Everything becomes wonderful, anything can be achieved, and then the honeymoon ends, and they revert back to "type".

Nothing is set in stone, and people can change from day to day. This is a very important and a basic principle in Pythagorean numerology. However, it is equally true that there IS a core 'type' that a person vibrates to, and that they both associate with others who share a similar (or opposite) frequency, and that they will return to this core energy again and again throughout their life.

Interpretations are on the following pages. Please read through them carefully, and be aware that no one person is purely any single "type".

Positive/Active Life Path

The Positive/active Mode is, generally, a joy to behold. It is not the highest ideal, which is always a mix of all the character traits and modes of expression, but it is certainly a strong and purposeful step in the right direction of integration.

It has a certain childlike sense of wonder and curiosity that is great fun at parties. It is good at sniffing out the curious and different aspects of life. These are the people you meet when you travel off on your own to the top of some distant peak.

However, life is basically full of contradiction and opposition. This type also tend not to compromise, and thus create waves wherever they go. Even when they hold no ill will or bad intention, people will read negative patterns into their actions.

Why is this so? I find that people locked into lesser spaces tend to judge a person from their own viewpoint. "If I were to do this, it would mean I think that!" The Negative/Passive type, in particular, really get stirred up by the Positive/Active type.

People locked into conservative beliefs and social dogmas get the impression that the Positive/Active persona considers itself superior to them. It appears to the conservative that they practice socially unacceptable behavior. The paradox, of course, is that the person with the issue is the one with the problem. Life tends to be like this: whatever a person exhibits and perceives as a fault in others, is usually their own.

A classic case is the opposition to Julius Caesar by the "boni", or traditionalists, throughout his political career. They hated everything he represented. Caesar is the perfect example of the pure Positive/Active life path.

Children between Ages 4 to 7 generally move through the Positive/Active expression mode. They are finding their feet, and are able to look after themselves to a small degree. Mother becomes less an issue of survival, and more one of comfort. Father becomes something the mind can engage, rather than a distant image of dominance. The child is connecting with the world, making decisions, and asking questions.

They believe they are past the need for boundaries and are now into exploring their natural limits.

It is a wonderful period or confidence and freedom for the child, if they are allowed to express themselves. Then it begins to change. The child starts to interact with society more and more, and their confidence can be eroded. The need to be accepted and to fit in can take over. This is where the Positive/Active state can switch to any of the other four states, as the Soul chooses alternative ways to best survive on this planet.

However, if we look at young children, they just want to grow, to live, and to experience life. Uncluttered by compromise, or the social restraints, they ask the big "Why" of life and look closely at the answers they receive back. They grow "as the Lilies in the field".

This world has a strong negative tendency, as emphasized by the fact that gravity is always pushing us down. It makes us strong, of course, but many get worn down by the constant pressure. However, the Positive/Active Mode will see this as a challenge rather than an obstacle. Nothing dents them, nothing stops them, everything is possible.

All top businessmen, athletes and people who excel in their fields are carrying strong Positive/Active traits. This type is marked with a healthy sense of curiosity and adventure, and given the choice, they go for constant change rather than repetitive behavior. This energy always drives the person on to the next, bigger, brighter horizon.

Clearly, this type can become too over weighted with the positive, and actually have a negative effect on relationships and those around them. They simply are too busy forging ahead to listen. As always, there is a question of balance, and integrating to some degree the qualities of ALL types into a singular mode of expression.

There is a natural arrogance with the Positive/Active type. It starts as a "can do" attitude, but when it becomes clear that many can't do, the person under the influence of this energy stream tends to inflate giving themselves a greater importance. In this sense, around them they encourage the Positive/Passive energy. This starts growing in people around them, and the "silent" battle that ensues (usually in relationships) can poison the pure spirit of these people.

There is a real art to understanding how the differing energies come in to play and distort the natural flows, but one thing that is simple, what distorts is always a passion that is out of control in a person. Even the passion for excellence can drive a person beyond the natural boundaries where they fit in with society, and thus over weighted with this driving force, the energy in the person distorts in the persona.

This distortion is actually a tear in the auric structure, where negatives such as fear, guilt and loneliness open up the inner consciousness to alternative 'feedlines' of energy. This, by the way, is the main reason for the Buddhist adherence to the principle of right association, and this is the natural reason WHY there is a class structure.

We go into this area of thought under "The Law of Association"

If we fail to recognize that ALL polarities attract their natural opposites energy fields. then all modes of existence will become difficult. Again, refer back to the "cog" diagram of the introductory section.

The Positive/Active type will attract the Negative/Passive type and, until both aspects learn to integrate, every move you make is like selecting gears without using the clutch.

Naturally, both aspects are within ourselves, but we will attract this externally as well. I had a neighbor once who just seemed to oppose anything I did on a property. It made no sense, because much of what I did was a benefit to himself as well, but he blindly opposed everything.

The matter went to the Supreme Court, with the Chief Justice asking his counsel why we were even here? They could provide no answer.

It is a perfect example of what happens when the Positive/Active meets the Negative/Passive. The agent for change meets the agent for no-change.

It is the same question of "What happens when an immovable object meets an irresistible force" In simple terms, one takes on the energy field of the other. In my case, I started to become negative and moody, while the opposing, immobile force became aggressive and arrogant. We both took on the character traits we disliked in the other.

However, I recognized what was happening, and by accepting and integrating the energy within myself, the opposition began to fade, and it opened new doorways in my life. Things like this book you now hold came about because of it. And that is just how it is.

We need to be ourselves, yet, in order to climb the hills and enjoy the highways better, we also need to be able to synchronize with others . And here is a curious thing. The negative character aspects are much better at synchronizing with other negatives than positives with positives. It is a curious thing, but there is a strong survival talent in the negative principle.

We take this subject up in chapter on Synchronicity in Ratology: Way of the Un-dammed

What the Positive/Active type needs to learn most is patience. We see this type beating the drums of war when there is opposition to their plans, and the problem is, they tend to create wars as a result.

If this type can learn patience, they also tend to pick up the "four C's": Character, Courtesy, Charm and Class. At least, you would hope so.

The bull at the gate is OK in an open field, but in the china shop of emotions, this type creates havoc and disturbance, and become their own worst enemies. The funny thing is, with this type the belief usually is: if you just push harder, it will all come right.

If patience and balance is not leaned, these people become moody and take on depression and cynical attitudes as baggage in old age. Dreams become memories, and often these people turn to drug and alcohol abuse in order to sustain their personality.

Or they flip completely, and move into the Positive/Passive mentality. Here you often find this type as the power broker, the dealer, the politician and the ambitious types that are prepared to walk over people to get what they want.

And what is more, when the Positive/Active shifts to this mode, they are generally VERY successful. They are not necessarily happy, but they certainly attain a high degree of success in their chosen field.

In this case, the "Messiah" image comes to the fore, and a wonderful, magnetic smile can be used to embrace all who enter into the psychic field of the person. This type literally charms the pants, and sometimes the bank balance, off others.

Another aspect of this is when the person turns to become the inveterate "do-gooder". This is a characteristic of someone who failed at balancing their Positive/Active intentions and found a clever way to control a situation.

The last flip of this aspect is with the Manipulator. This is the out and out controller.

More interestingly, and it is a curious thing, it is the case where ALL the above tend to attract the Negative/Passives to them like moths to a flame.

A typical failed Positive/Active is Hitler and Mussolini. Many people who become church and political leaders are also in this category. The saying that characterizes the failed Positive/Active is: "Surely the good shepherd lives to fleece his flock, but just as surely the flock loves to be shorn"

Or as Marlene Dietrich sang "Boys gather to me like moths around a flame, and if they get their wings burnt, then who am I to blame?"

In the sustained positive/active aspect, there is little interest in the person having a flock that follows, unless it helps achieve specific ends. The focus is more on attaining goals and attaining successful outcomes for self and family.

Negative/Active Life Path

This is an interesting, if quite difficult path to follow. It is rightfully called "The Poet's Path" and it tends to attract the dreamers, the musicians as well as the vagabonds and spiritual nere-do-wells.

These people tend to live on the outskirts of respectability, and are classed as "bohemian" in the more positive aspect, and as drunks and useless bums in the negative.

I met a wonderful character of this type in the streets of Sydney. He was an alcoholic, and told me his story. He became a solicitor because daddy made sure of it, but he hated telling lies and living a deceitful life. He became depressed and eventually ended up an alcoholic in the street, and far happier as a result. It was a classic case of a child not allowed to express their creative energy. This man was a natural poet, and the Negative/Active path is all about expressing your creative energy.

Few grasp this, but the creative force comes through the negative emotions, as a rule. It is the inward, introspective, self-questioning energy that seeks out and finds ways to solve the state of opposition inside themselves, usually through art or similar.

Yet woe to them that succeed. One of the hardest things for a person under this life path to do is to be happy with success. Success tends to depress them, and they take up damaging personal habits to circumvent having to deal with their achievements.

Doesn't this sound ridiculous? It is how it is. This lot tend to be foot shooters until they learn to get their level of EXPRESSION above their level of introversion.

One artist I knew, a genuine genius, was offered early on in his career $25000 for a piece. This was ten time the price anyone had offered in the past, but my friend refused it, saying "It is worth twice that!"

Regardless of the fact that accepting the offer at that time would have set a new profile for him that would have indeed started pushing his prices up to twice the offer, he shot himself in the foot because the external reality of success still didn't match his inner dream of struggle, failure and difficulty.

This is often the problem with creative people. While on one hand they would be happy for pennies to be able to eat that day, the other side insists that the "vision splendid" requires suffering. It is the tension between the commercial reality and the creative ideal that imprisons this life path. (Numerically a 3-4 opposition) Until the person gets a handle on this, they stay behind the eight ball of negative circumstance.

Many of the this path reject social standards, and fall into a deep depression we call the Dark Night of the Soul. This is an archetypal period most of us go through at some time, and be assured, you are going through the Negative/Active phase at some point.

It is only when you start calling this darkness your friend that you get STUCK in this mode of expression. When your paranoia becomes your best friend, watch out.

An overview of someone locked in this phase, which is really meant to be a transitory phase for creative purposes, gives us an image of a small person confined by tragedy. Everything they touch turns to lead, no one appreciates their genius, yet they remain forthright and firm in their creative task.

The life of Vincent Van Gogh is a classic example of someone stuck in this phase. When he became an evangelical minister, he broke out of this for a time, but the deeper calling dragged him back to the Negative/Active life path. It was a painful existence for Van Gogh, yet a life that created some of the most remarkable art ever produced.

We see this mode in children, especially with the dreamers and those who forget to do the basic things of the everyday. The dishes pile up, the clothes are unwashed, but give them the latest computer game, and watch them click over to Positive/Active in a flash!

It is actually perfectly natural to flick between Positive/Active and Negative/Active. Harmonically this is like the Major and Minor mode of any given Key. But what happens is that the Minor Key can be somewhat intoxicating with its sweet sadness, and we can get trapped in what seems the beauty of the moment.

For a time, when I was 16, I wrote very sad poetry. What happened next was that I started feeling sad. This was not my natural nature at all, and I wondered why. I looked at what I was expressing, and realized that I had clicked myself into this Negative/Active way of being because of the type of creative work I was expressing.

I changed what I wrote and I instantly cheered up. Curiously, my artist friend, the one who refused the $25K, always writes songs in the minor key!

As an addendum to that story, he finally found the woman he loved, married her, and settled into produce his finest work. Not just that, he finishes these in weeks rather than years as was the norm in the past. That's the switch to Positive/Active.

What happened to break the Negative/Active cycle he was in? It was so simple. He gave some work away, including copyright, to a spiritual organization he was a member of. This action broke the "Minor" spell that held him, and allowed a greater degree of inner success, and reality, to enter his heart. Now, even his guitar work is more upbeat.

A problem with this mode of expression is that, as a child, other children would pick this and see it as a vulnerability. So they start attacking. Children are like this, they prey on what seems the vulnerable, trying to find an opening to make someone squeal.

As a result, these folk develop a shield around their "sensitive" areas, and often build up elaborate conversations with themselves in order to cover the hurt they feel. It is a curious process where we feel we are protecting what is sacred inside us, but where, in reality we are simply erecting walls and cutting ourselves off from communication.

The thing to remember here is something terribly simple. *It takes the same amount of bricks and the same amount of effort to build a bridge as it does to build a wall.* We all have a little of this mode inside us, and so we all need to remember this.

The Romantic, the Gypsy, and the Tall Silent Type. All of these are evidence of the Negative/Active persona at work. This mode has a deep sense of alternating current, and can go from deep introspection to open hearted laughter in a moment. Harmonically speaking it is the Major/Minor modulation. And this is a blessing as well as a curse.

It breaks up the moodiness the individual feels, but it also makes it hard for those around them to feel they are connecting in some meaningful way, leaving partners and friends with an odd sense that this person cannot really be trusted.

Book of Number: Client Psychology

In truth, the Negative/Active type tend to be the most trustworthy of all the Querent Modes, and yet the most misunderstood, and unappreciated. They have a dog-like devotion for those who care for them, but along with this can come an intensity that tends to drive a wedge between communication.

These folk are destined to much heart-break and disappointment in the area of human relations, at least until they stop the sense of being insular and withdraw, and learn to trust their partner enough to share their fears and anxieties. Sharing releases mush of the negative "charge" in these mode.

Intimacy is what they crave, and fear. Opening up to the universe is their desire, and yet like any good horror movie, they always expect something terrible to happen if they do.

This creates an inner turmoil that stirs up the creative forces. The creative effort causes the pain to subside, and so the individual can become a "creative Junkie". The net result is fascinating: They cause havoc in order to get the creative 'fix' they love.

This type tend to be would-be if could-be hermits. They would really love to leave it all behind, but the coffee smells too good at the cafe'. The other classic typecast here is the person who is always going to write the greatest book, paint the most important painting, sing the best song, etc. They would, if they could, but they don't.

The strange mechanism at work here is that the negative pressure has to get so strong that they "collapse" into actually performing or creating a work. Otherwise they will procrastinate and avoid the inner conflict they both detest and adore. As a result, these folk are somewhat self-destructive. The creative pursuit tends to be somewhat fatalistic and until these folk discover a sense of their own value, they appear to be pushed around by any wind the fates may send.

And yet, they are lucky. There always seems to be a meal or a bed with a person will to keep them warm. This "luck" is a natural thing, and is really the instinct of others to care for a child that the Negative/Active path brings out in others. Paradoxically, they will have a love-hate relationship with their mother, because they hate being mothered!

You will never make any sense of it, and neither can the person living inside this bubble. Just accept it, and allow the energy to move to it's next phase.

The life cycle of the Negative/Active life path is like alternating current. It switches back and forth, and in doing so creates the energy to burn the midnight candle. People affected by this Mode work best when connected to the earth in some way. Either actual gardening settles them, or they have an earthy friend, or similar.

Positive/Passive Life Path

Less than 5% of the people in any given society will carry a strong charge of this life path energy. But generally, if you meet them, they will be in influential positions. And you WILL meet them, so it is important to grasp the feel of this type, and know how to deal with them.

The Positive/Passive type tend to be the ones that explore their hidden desires, and can be quite secretive. They can work to the greater good, or merely to serve themselves, or they will do both with equal vigor. They can run the Cat Protection Society as well as the local whore house without blinking an eye at the apparent contradiction.

The 'rules' this life path follows can be quite curious. The First Rule is, generally, to give people enough rope to hang themselves. These folk will play out a role in order to bait someone to give them information, which they will then use against the individual. The Second Rule is based on what seems the natural distrust this type suffers: Never offer too much information about themselves in a given situation, unless it is necessary.

This type generally cannot trust others, and usually the Positive/Passive type have had hard experiences that lead them to this state of distrust. But, as a result, they often do well in business and areas where distrust is an asset.

You will find many Asian Brides, who will do anything to improve the quality of their life, fit this category. They may act passive to attract a mate, yet they are very domineering.

The type as a whole can be typified as "The Rebel without a Cause". Usually they have a covert (or overt) need for power and/or money. This need tends to tip them over the scale of courtesy and respect and become VERY self serving.

These are the space invaders: the ones who step over other people's boundaries and trample the flowers. Why? Purely to establish who is boss.

It is a curious and complex life path. People with it often start out with a deep distrust that is based on some negative on their past, and then they flip and can counter this distrust with an obsessive need to help others. It can all grow to an odd form of manipulation that causes much grief in personal relationships. "I have done so much for you, yet you still treat me badly" is the common song this type sings.

The Positive/Passive are calculating. They will quietly count all the things they have done for you, and remind you of things they claim you said last year, in order to put themselves in a position of authority. They will keep mental notes for years about someone, and cherish the notion of a revenge (all in good time) secretly in their hearts.

Of course, they win some and lose some, but in all ways they alienate themselves from others, and create for themselves deep degrees of loneliness. All this because they cannot trust another or, more importantly, they cannot trust life loves them. The result is invariably a loss of face, a loss of position, and a degree of misery: all directly as a result of the manipulating schemes they make and the games they have played.

The extraordinary thing is that this type are invariably blind to the causation of events that lead to these events. Rather they will see everything going wrong as a proof of their innate distrust. The ONLY cure for the negative mind games of this type is to learn to trust life to provide what they need. A big ask, considering they tend to believe that self-sufficiency is core to happiness.

At heart what this type of individual is really looking for is simply to find a place of security for themselves. And yet, almost every time, they have to lose everything before they recognize this. It seems the pattern, that this life path only understands their failings when it is too late, and their life is in ruins.

This is when they can become REALLY dangerous!

At this point, they pick themselves up and make a choice. Get over it, get a life, and learn to interact with others in a natural way: Or, seek more control.

If they choose the control path, watch out. These folk can be utterly ruthless. If they dispose of the desire to help others entirely, they begin to enjoy hurting others to get what they want. It can become quite sadistic.

This type are the true witches and warlocks, if you will. They are shape shifters who project mind energy to shape the world into the form they want it to be, and they will literally say and do whatever it takes to get the objects of their desire.

This aspect of the life path energy is very duplicitous. It will mimic caring for others, but only as a tool to boost the personal self-esteem The mental justification for their innate arrogance is: I must be better than that person, because they need my help.

Inertia with the Positive/Passive Life Path

We all justify our own actions to ourselves in some degree. Yet this is never more evident than with the Positive/Passive mode. The person affected by this energy almost always has large blinkers on to help them stop seeing the effects of their actions. What is more, they really see themselves as forging their own path in life, whereas what the energy is really doing is stepping over others, and barreling along with a sort of inertia.

Everything we do creates inertia, which is to say, the effect of our previous actions will push forward and drive the present action. This is called the Samsara, the flow of images that build into the picture we inhabit. We appear to be going with a natural flow, and we are, but that does not mean it is what is best for us. The Positive/Passive innately knows this, and so goes out of it's way to control external realities.

With the Positive/Passive, the Passive aspect will go with the flow, while the Positive aspect narrows the focus to manipulate this flow to the best ends that serve itself.

The net result is often the mindset becomes "What can I get from this situation"

Many of the writers and artists who speak on social issues, and who stress correcting social wrongs, are following this Life Path. They like to appear altruistic, and caring. On one level, they are, but at heart they are counting what they will get.

These folk generally offer a hint of their personal persecution in their art and writing. Mein Kamph is a perfect example of the Positive/Passive persona at work. In the guise of building a greater Germany, Hitler was plotting to make himself the sole arbiter of its fate. David Niven hinted about this type in "The Moons a Balloon" when he defined a gentleman as "a courteous bastard".

This type always have a strong suicidal tendency. This death-wish usually shifts sideways into a desire for strong drink or powerful mind altering drugs. They generally have a strong enough personality to hold off the worst effects of their own destructive natures, and often they do this for many years. But eventually, the burden of self-loathing wears them down, and when the fatigue sets in, the hidden demons emerge.

Life's focus becomes blurred, and they will drift in and out of states of despair. Yet, weirdly enough, this can make them more attractive to passive aggressive, who will most conveniently live off the energy evoked, and then blame them, for making their life difficult when it all falls apart.

They are hard to live with and impossible to make headway with in any argument. The Positive/Passive type can be a complete pig, one who offends everyone at a party, then the next day be as sweet as apple pie, leaving people wondering what they did wrong to upset the poor soul! True! I have seen it happen.

This mode loves power. Their main issue is their own inner barriers, their own sense of restriction. So the native feels that in order to be powerful they must break down all barriers and go where the angels fear to tread. He who dares, wins. In the extreme, these are the Hitler's of society, but generally they are the money merchants, the Mafioso, the religious leaders: High profile people in high profile jobs.

When you are driven to excel, the first thing you realize is that you cannot excel under the thumb of another. This mode is driven to get away from their own inner torment by succeeding in some manner. Success is their proof of personal worth.

On the flip side, this energy line is also responsible for many of the highly spiritual beings in our society. Many of the Saints were driven individual who directed their efforts to a higher purpose. They used the Passive aspect to look inward, and the Positive aspect to strive for truth. So as you can see, there is no fixed rule of good or bad for any type: Just a tendency to follow certain paths.

The Positive aspect of this type is a genuine need to care for others, and to help them, but as mentioned, the energy can go overboard and these people can become inveterate do-gooders and act in ways that are completely interfering to others.

When the individual realizes they are acting in this way in order to avoid dealing with a conflict inside themselves, they have a chance of balancing this energy out. They can become very useful members of society at this point.

Side Bar: General Considerations

Of course, there is no 'absolute' purity of any one type in any one person. We are all a mix of all types, but we do tend to have a majority of focus on one type.

Even so: It is very rare to see a Positive/Active type revert to a Positive/Negative. But it can, and does, happen when extreme pressure is brought upon the person. They will pick up the passive energy to avoid conflict, and then sublimate the conflict into a curious aggression that will act to keep perceived danger away.

This is what little dogs do to protect themselves. They act big and mean, and tough. Often other dogs keep their distance, because they look too much a bother.

At the absolute root of ALL the Life Paths, there is a choice to act for either love, or power. The Positive/Passive type have this question more prevalent than others. Certainly, if they are to find peace on this planet, it is a question they need to sort out.

As much as a Positive/Active type can revert to a Positive/Passive under pressure, so too can the Positive/Passive revert to a Negative/Passive if it all gets too much.

Achievement, or success of some sort, is necessary in ALL modes for the individual to feel comfortable in their own skin. However. it is **absolutely essential** in both the Positive/Active and Positive/Passive life paths for the individual to be able to look in the mirror and like what they see.

Artistic integrity and deep cultural insight can be held by the people under this life path, but they tend to be their own worst enemy, as a rule. Instead of creating great literature, they would prefer to hire someone to write the story. It is a difficult aspect, and in the end the decision of the individual directions is really is between the choice to follow love or power as the guiding light.

The fact that most choose power is more an indication of the weight and tendency of this world than that of the life path. But then again, someone needs to run the place!

It needs to be understood that in cases, such as with Osama Bin Laden, how powerfully the Positive/Passive energy can be. This energy can literally take over the mental power of others. As an example: Bin Ladin's followers were dominated by HIS ideals, yet they believed them to be their own. The ones that flew the planes into the World Trade Center were classic Positive/Passive Types, ruled by the stronger mind. The energy was such they truly would feel glory and joy in their suicide for a cause. The Bin Ladin types know this, and use it to their personal benefit.

We are all ruled by three core forces: building, sustaining, and destruction. The Positive/Passives are the type to kick over the sand-castle that someone else built. Why? To show you that they can.

The trick to successfully navigating this energy is to move into the present moment, and to experience the natural flow of life. If you are to avoid the negative inertia, what we might call bad karma, then our attitude has to be one of genuine service. When we hold this, the Positive/Passive life path takes on a saint-like clarity, and you can truly assist others to a better place, as well as yourself.

Negative/Passive Life Path

The Negative/Passive's are by far the largest of all the Querent groups. These are the "sheep" and really they have the mentality of the lamb to the slaughter. This type just want Christmas dinner, some friends, and a good time with the family. But if life sends them down the hard road, they just accept the fate in store. They will walk to to the chopping block, all the time complaining to the other lambs beside them of their lot.

It is a pattern that belongs to the herd mentality, plagued by the evils of gossip and low self-esteem, and the other thousand assorted problems that follow on from these.

This sounds as if it is negative, and the truth is that it is. But this is OK. This type form the basic workers that provide the product and services that society needs. They are run by the Positive/Active and Positive/Passive types, as a rule, and are not the type to even want to be the directors of their own fate, or the captain of their destiny.

A good job, a good time, a nice partner, a few kids and this life path is genuinely happy and content. They like being an indian, and are perfectly happy when they have what they consider to be a reasonable and fair chief telling them what to do.

What is more, it is VERY important that we understand that this is perfectly OK. The fisherman who likes nothing better than a drink after hours at the bar, the wife who is happy balancing the family budget: These people will never be given Academy Awards, but they ARE the backbone of society and are the reason why those who DO receive awards and accolades can. Because, without this life path, there is no audience.

Does this seem demeaning? The Ego loves to strut the stage as the lead actor, but no actor can succeed without an audience. The only real problem the Negative/Passive has is when the people in charge become overbalanced in the Positive/Passive life path.

(Classically, tyrants such as Saddam Hussein, and Mussolini and Hitler are typical of all that can go wrong in society. This is when the Positive/Passive energy that chooses power as its goal gains ascendancy over a population.)

Democracy is supposed to hand power to the people, however the real facts are that the people vote in accordance to the carrot that is offered. Politicians and media tend to rule the minds of the Negative/Passive, but if they powers that be go too far, and turn the masses against them, this life path turns on them with great cruelty.

When you push the Negative/Passive individual too far it creates an anger whirlpool that, as a group, is virtually unstoppable. The Polish resistance, the ending of Communism, these are examples of ordinary people polarizing and galvanizing into a force of the people for the people. It is the force of change when organized and directed.

The Romans knew this force well. They made sure the local populace was distracted with games, and other things. Keep the common people from becoming a mob! Their philosophy of "Divide and Conquer" is what allowed them to stay in power for so long.

The happiest path of the Negative/Passive is one of contemplation. Living close to the land, having an agreeable group of fellows about them, and living life from day to day is the pattern that works best for this life path. If communist governments allow the peasants to earn enough, and have enough entertainment, they succeed because this type find this arrangement quite suitable.

Book of Number: Client Psychology

Of course, negative passions stir is the hearts of all men and women, and as this force enters it seeks specifically to shake up calm and peaceful lifestyles. So in essence, if you have someone who seems clearly in the Negative/Passive group the best thing to do is to help reinforce the ideals of Charity, Friendship and Harmony along with the simple notion of gratitude and doing a good deed every day.

This is an easy life path to follow. Yet oddly enough we meet some HIGHLY advanced Souls who have chosen this lifetime to live it. You may seem surprised, but the external life path of a person is not their spiritual power. There are some 'simple' housewives that are deep reservoirs of peace and calm, for instance. Some 'common' workers offer, through simple common sense, a view that can help a company remain productive, and thus indirectly help pay the wages of hundreds of men and women.

This type is not a star that burns fiercely in the night sky, but when you considered the cost of being a star is to be alone unto yourself, perhaps being ordinary makes sense.

You will not find many stars in this group, but you WILL find MANY good people who know the value of simple friendship and honest effort. These are the Salt of the Earth, the farmers, the producers. the small businessmen.

The greatest problem this group suffers is the fear of success, which they feel will alien-ate them from their fellows. Curiously, most children start out in the Positive/Active category, but end up in the Negative/Passive life path. Why? Generally, they feel lonely when they are alone. It is that simple.

So, logically, if someone wants to lift out of the Negative/Passive life path, and raise themselves to a different standard, they need to learn to be "Alone but not Lonely".

It is that simple. Along with this, naturally, a person needs to educate themselves with a skill that can carry themselves in society and allow them a degree of personal freedom. On this "changeover" of life path you will find the tradesman who becomes a craftsman or anyone who truly masters the vocation, or calling, they follow.

Research into Soccer Pools winners in England came up with fascinating statistics. All but three people in the Lower Classes who won large pay-outs in the pools were WORSE OFF after five years. The three that were OK were a woman, who left the money to her cats. A Priest, who gave a good part of it away, and a fellow who got smart, invested and made himself more money.

The rest spent it, gave it away, and suffered divorce, alienation from their friends and untold negatives from such an apparent stroke of good fortune. That is the way of the Negative/Passive. They are like the bug that the spider sets a web for, and society has may spiders and many webs to catch the unwary.

We may call it the "great unwashed" the "lower classes" and tyrants may use these peo-ple as cannon fodder in their wars, but the fact remains, these are the people that cause society to function. This life path has no real desire to be a big shot in the local show, or to look more important than the next person, and they may not have a million dollars in the bank: But if this life path simply stays with common sense and respect for another person's rights, then they do fine in this lifetime.

The Nothing Trap

All the Querent Modes can be swallowed up in what the writer of the "Never Ending Story" called "The Nothing Trap"

This is an area where the imagination dies because the individual has become too caught up in the material world.

The person will exhibit cynical and pointless observations about people, judgmental attitudes, and a distinct sense of a silent apathy. Their actions are more of the walking dead than the living, because nothing seems to hold the promise of a brighter tomorrow. Drug and/or alcohol abuse tend to become habitual.

If someone has fallen into this, you will see the fatalistic look in their eye, and there is really nothing you can do for them. They need hope, and something to look forward to, so the best suggestion you can make is for them to make a complete break from their present surroundings. Suggest they go on a long holiday, go hiking in the Himalayas, or do something completely different to what they presently are doing.

Just get active while doing interesting thing.

The Harmonic Mode

It must also be said that there is a "Harmonic Mode" that is a gestalt of all the four Querent Modes. This resonates with the Number 12, and is a Master Vibration that many may touch, but few will manage to stabilize in their day to day lives.

This mode indicates that a person has moved completely into the serenity of their own beingness, and these folk are rare indeed. This serenity is quite peculiar in that it allows the person to apparently break the spiritual and traditional laws and suffer no consequence of the action. It is because they simply move in accordance with the harmonic song, or energy, that guides them.

In a sense, in this mode you can do no wrong.

Cato the Elder is a good example of this state of being. When he was cast out of Rome by the Emperor Nero, this was considered at the time as a punishment worse than death. Cato was asked how he felt, what would he do? He replied simply "I will leave, in my own way."

In other words, the worst possible thing had befallen him, yet he was unmoved and would quietly go about his business in the way he saw fit.

As a result, he seeded an entire generation with the principles of BEINGNESS.

"Thus by doing nothing, the sage teaches all" (Lao Tsi)

HOW TO APPLY THE FOUR QUERENT MODES IN REAL LIFE

ntellectual understanding and practical application are often poles apart. What we need to do is practice picking the type of mode a person you meet may be in. Being right or wrong is not the point. It is learning to PERCEIVE where someone is at, and where they are coming from, that matters.

Why? The best predictor of future performance is past results.

Without judging, try looking at people you meet in the street and about town. Look and get a feel for where they are at. If you can, start trying to pick the Querent Modes that are active in them. As you practice this, you generate a "thought field" or a type of magnetism whereby you begin to recognize things you never saw before.

It is a little like when you buy a Volkswagen Beetle. You never really noticed them, but suddenly you seem to see them everywhere. More importantly, as you focus on where others are at, you in turn begin to get a feel for where YOU are at. Without thinking, you will start to realize what type of energy you are channeling, and by being aware of this, you will find ways of directing it. It is all about being HERE-NOW.

All Four Modes align internally when we are HERE-NOW. This is the Harmonic Mode. When you attain this deep presence of mind in regards yourself, you find that people will naturally respect your view, and listen more to what you have to say.

Being HERE-NOW does NOT mean nothing changes. Watch yourself as you go through the differing phases, because you will experience every one of them several times every day. And more amazingly watch your clients as they come in. Just observe, without saying anything. Just pause, wait, see, and then you will find things go "click". When the client subconsciously realizes they have been recognized, watch them shift gears. When a person is "seen" they enter the role they play with their dominant parent figure.

It is a fascinating thing to observe. When someone KNOWS they have been seen, so much dishonesty falls away, and they stand before you naked, in a sense. The earnest ones will love you for it, and feel free. The ones that want to hide behind their masks, you will never see again.

I lost a really well paid job because of this. The wife of the boss came in, and was chatting about their forthcoming move to London. I watched, and saw her inherent sense she felt of wasting her life as a mere housewife. I asked a few simple questions about her goals when she got there, and by her answers, she revealed to both myself and herself that she was deeply unhappy. She was really a base Active/Positive, but playing a Passive/Positive role to please her husband.

When she realized I had seen this, she just looked at me. She said nothing, but I was fired that afternoon, without cause. It happens. I guess it gave me some more stories to tell about how going hungry can sharpen the mind! The truth indeed will set you free, but it won't necessarily pay the bills.

Next we look at the Survival Scale.

The Survival Scale

Every person lives on a sliding scale of internal survival. The lowest point is death, the highest point is serenity of being-ness. Naturally, we oscillate between what we call negative and positive areas on this scale. This is called the Tone Scale in Scientology, but it has other names in other teachings, and really it is something that is very obvious. People have either a life-wish, or a death-wish, controlling them.

Recognizing something is one thing, and fairly simple, but getting a client to understand this is more difficult. There is a powerful technique you can use to communicate the simplicity of this notion: Give the client a graph with the highest of emotions down to the lowest down the left hand side, and a time period broken into half hours on the horizontal axis. Ask them to mark where they feel they are "at" every 1/2 hour for four days. (We have these available at Number Harmonics, if you care to purchase some.)

When it comes down to it, people are either working towards their death-wish or their life-wish. Generally it is a bit of a mix between the two. The death-wish is noted through the habits that come with it: Smoking, drinking, drug usage, indulgence in mood or food, excess reliance of pharmaceuticals, etc. These are some of the manifestations of the death-wish. When people see a graph of where they are at emotionally, it often sets the mood for them to consider what they can do to change things.

If you get an understanding of where a client is at on the life/death wish scale, which is really the Survival Scale, you can work with them far more easily.

A Life Wish is evidence by a bright nature. There is a generally optimistic outlook and a sense that whatever the obstacle, it will be gotten over. Generally, you do not see these types for a reading about what they want to "get", but often it is about whether a new partner is suitable, or when they are looking for spiritual guidance or inspiration.

The person carrying a Death Wish has certain traits. Almost invariably they ask about a lost love, or will they find their perfect partner, or will something go their way, that sort of thing. Emotions are the driving force.

The Death Wish motivation tends towards control of a situation whereas the Life Wish motivation is more about how to can get over a particular pattern that is often already recognized. The Death Wish tends to have the Emotions as the driving force, while the Life Wish people tend to have the Mind as the driving force.

It is important to note that both of these energies tend to be in constant conflict within each individual. The life-wish is more the call of Soul, trying to get through to the human consciousness. The death-wish is based more in the mental and emotional issues, and tends to arise mostly from the social and familial programming that came about through some negative experience or restricted upbringing. (the collective "shoulds")

What is VERY important to understand is that you must always allow whatever it is they wish to be. It is NOT for the practitioner to seek to alter or change the persona or inner direction of the client. It is important to know where someone is at, yes. This means we can better communicate on a level the person ill understand, but there should at no time be any wish to change or alter an individual. We are here to provide options.

Book of Number: Client Psychology

The Law of Karma states: We choose our parents and all the major turning points in our life have been pre-selected either through Soul's choice, or Karma. This does not mean the CHOICES we make are pre-determined, but the situations are. SO! What you as the Numerologist is best advised to do, is to highlight what options and choices are available to the client. We simply assist them in the arena of choice.

If someone gains great upliftment from a Numerical reading, it is because their life wish has taken a hold of the meaning behind the words, and run with it. In other words, Soul has managed to get a run for a few moments in that person's life. If they do not, you either did a poor job, or they didn't want what you offered.

So often the chart is perfectly clear about the direction to take, yet it seems that the person virtually refuses to do the obvious. They do not follow through on a choice that would so clearly have been a benefit to them, and for years I wondered why. Now I know: You can be assured that the death-wish has been selected, and this is generally ruled and governed by what we call the Censor. (Go To: The Censor)

As a short example, I have a woman come to me, asking about a move to another part of the country. I asked some questions, and it became clear the reason for the move was based on the fact that her boyfriend was moving, and she wanted to go along.

The numbers panned out very clearly that this would be a disastrous shift, but you cannot say this to a client. Rather, I pointed out the advantages of remaining where she was, and highlighted the fact that the move was one of uncertainty at this point. I even suggested that she wait at least three months, to see if the relationship was stable and to see if the area she was contemplating moving to suited her.

She agreed with everything I said, and saw the complete sense in it. Yet the next day she moved. As I say, common sense is the guiding rule when offering any suggestion to a client, but the fact is, their Censor will instruct them what to do. So, accept that often their death-wish will be the main driving force. We just have to allow for it.

I might add, if you make ANY absolute pronouncements, you are liable to be sued or slandered. Use words like: *perhaps consider this*, or, *the possibility here is*, that sort of language. Stay very neutral, never seek to change a situation, and remain within the boundaries of common sense. You will make more friends and less trouble. You will also function more effectively, and be of greater benefit to the client.

A person will make what they will of the work you do. Your work will never be perfect, nor will the acceptance of the client be absolute. However, by being careful not to activate a negative survival pattern in the client (where they feel cornered) and by keeping comments within a defined area of general observation and consideration, you stand a better chance of communicating what is essential in the chart.

The Jesuits insinuated themselves into Medieval society by ingratiating themselves to the Royal houses. They did this by making rational excuses for the necessity of the occasional atrocity, and generally relieving guilt from the shoulders of their flock.

The goal was to make the parishioner more God-like, thus it was seen as necessary not to contradict the Devil in them, but to allow and educate it. In a sense, it was a practice that won the day, and brought the Jesuits to the top of the Catholic Tree.

MEDIA

Religion and superstition have traditionally ruled the mind of Man, but now other forces have come into play. The above were the Media of the Middle Ages but now Science is the new religion, and both TV and the Web are worshipped.

Science, TV and the Web are the new media. These are the main vehicles of communication to the mass mind. Magazines, books, you say? Forget them. (but not this one!)

Even so, it is a curious fact that though very few people read anymore, they will believe that something is printed in a book is more credible than something spoken of in the daily TV news, or newspaper. You may have imagined, given the vastly larger viewership, that it should be the exact opposite, but it is not.

Anyone who has contact with running commercial media knows what absolute nonsense the bulk of what we call news is on TV. Yet, unless they physically read something that opposes this, the majority of people accept it as truth, and act accordingly. Most do not read books or look for information that offers anything beyond amusement, so public media tends to rule, and the real information in books is largely ignored.

How dangerous is this ignorance? In a word: Very. If a TV station reports that the head of a government agency made a negative comment about the economy, the economy dips in accordance to this. For example: Intel lost hundreds of millions of dollars on a media snip that said its new Pentium Chip was faulty. The fault was so minute that it was barely worth mentioning, in that the chip would make an error every 1000 years or so. But that comment almost wiped Intel from the stock market!

Right or wrong, media is powerful. It is a nonsense that media should hold so much power, yet it does. Why? Because most of the population is completely ignorant of anything outside of their immediate sphere of influence. As a rule, media shapes what is acceptable and true in society, and as a result, in turn most thought is shaped by it.

People are pulled this way and that by media, science, religion, superstition, programmed social codes, etc. And the strange part is that should you tell someone they are being ruled by external forces, or that their very thoughts are possibly not their own, they become very upset and attack you.

The reason I mention this is simple. As a trusted consultant you can sway people's opinions and thoughts. We need to stay within the boundaries of detachment and keep our comments to a clear minded commentary. What the client READS in their chart can have long, and powerful effects on them.

It is one of the issues I personally had to question when I started releasing so much of the Pythagorean teaching, such as you find here. It is likely that someone will misuse what they find in these pages. I would hope for otherwise, but I am a realist and know that some will not be able to help themselves, and will misuse the information. One thing I can assure you, if a person uses the spiritual truths to serve lower ideals, it is a boomerang that returns before this lifetime is done with.

In this category, the use of spiritual information to curry favor, gain prestige, or to enhance yourself in the eyes of another tends to bring about the opposite in the long term. To go further and abuse this information in order to make money or gain power over another will bring a swift response form the spiritual forces.

You, too, can fall into the trap of abusing media to gain control of people, or to get money from their wallets. But I promise you, this is a very expensive thing to do. You have every right to earn a decent living, of course. However, it pays to remember this simple truth:

When doing a Reading for another, YOU are the media. When you broadcast knowledge that can alter the shape of someone's life, you are the Media, and YOU are in a position of accountability and responsibility. How do we best shoulder this? It has been put very simply by a wise teacher.

The rule is as follows: **Care enough, to know enough, to do your very best.**

That's all you can do.

As you learn and gather the information of the Psychology of the Client, you will discover you hold levers to influence and sway almost anyone's opinion. If you can grasp the process by which Media influences the individual (Specifically in the area of the Censor) you will hold the tools to have almost anyone accept what you say as truth.

Suffice to say, Media in its present form is not that far removed from the use of so-called black magic. Advertisements are targeted to specific areas of the brain and psyche, and seek to alter a persons way of thinking to the benefit of the advertiser. A great deal of research is done on colour combinations, shelf placement, product shape and size, and all to induce a person to pick it up and put the thing into a trolley.

For you as a reader, there is a kind of backlash "zombie field" energy in the clients you will have to deal with. As they have been pummelled by images and inducements for so long, there is a kind of "dead zone" to cross before you can start waking them up to what you have to say.

You can use tricks, such as wearing a hood and cape and appearing mysterious, or you can use truth. Or both! Understanding where someone is coming from, connecting to this what they need to know, and giving them the freedom to accept or reject your view is the pure Pythagorean method.

But whatever works for you is what is right for you.

Next we come to what is possibly the hardest to grasp, yet most important study in this entire course: Understanding the Censor

The CENSOR

B asically, everyone you meet is stuck in a box. Yet how do I describe this box to a person living in It? "It has six flat sides, eight corners, and a lid." They say, as they can clearly see six sides and eight corners, "Of course it does, do you think I am an idiot!" Yet I can walk away and they are still in the box. If you can grasp and come to understand the contents of these pages, you will find a way out of the box.

We all have a creature inside us, a hidden Shadow Controller, the Censor, that secretly tells us what to do in every situation. Somerset Maugham, that marvelous teller of poignant short stories, has a section of one story where he unveils the Censor in full glory. It is placed against the tale of Satan seeking to tempt the Christ. The Devil tried three times to seduce Jesus, but when it appears he cannot win, Satan says "Oh well, I guess I will simply have to let you go so that you can die on the cross and save humanity"

As Jesus leaves, the Devil smiles, because he know the Messiah has fallen for his Forth Temptation. Cute hey? He is really describing how the Censor works in each of us. He gave Christ a temptation that appealed to the inner structure of his mind as being "right". The Censor, in effect, "bribes" us with life as we wish it to be seen, not as it is.

The Censor is a gestalt of all the images that form the collage we call our internal make-up. It is a powerful Director of Affairs who generally remains hidden in the dark side of our makeup. I saw it as a young man, clear as day, but did not understand exactly what it was. What I could see was that it somehow controlled me through my desires. (Which meant I spent many fruitless and unhappy years trying to eliminate desire.)

Eventually I learned it is easier and better to simply direct our energies to a useful purpose, thus putting our 'desires' to work and training this energy to follow more useful patterns. But this was much later. First I needed to come to grips with my Censor.

What cracked open the door to understanding this aspect of being that we all share came when I was traveling and researching. And the door was cracked open FOR me.

On one very specific occasion in the States, it was late at night and I was walking along Venice Beach in Los Angeles. With no warning, the spiritual forces saw fit to open my eyes (An act known as the Vidya, or True-Seeing) to the conditions that surrounded and controlled every person that walked down the crowded esplanade.

I saw in detail every habit, condition and "tag" that was part of each individual person. I saw clearly how it was served up as a collage of images that the person themselves thought was what they call "self". I could have easily gone up to anyone in the passing parade and described in complete detail every single thought they had in their makeup, every emotion they experienced, and every condition that ruled their heart and mind. I could even see where it came from: the mother, the society, etc.

However, I also came to realize that if I did this, the person would hate me for it. This is difficult to explain, but in simple terms, no one likes to feel naked before another unless they have a love connection. It would be like I came up and took their clothes off in public. People LIKE their blinkers and would feel unsafe without their "clothes" of thought and feeling, even though they are chains that hold them in place.

For many days after this, the resonance of the experience stayed with me. It radiated in waves of enormous power and if I spoke to anyone, I found they got extremely agitated.

On one occasion, at a party some fellow I did not know asked why I looked so unworldly (I gather he was asking for drugs) and I just started talking about this experience. Well, soon enough I had to leave the room. He started screaming at me, saying he couldn't believe how ANGRY I was. True, he was screaming and saying how angry "I" was!

Now, I have some clue as to how Spirit moves. Experiences like this tell me to look at my OWN lack of awareness of the structures that were holding MYSELF in place.

From this understanding I came to see that we ALL have a series of conditions that hold us in a fixed consciousness. The Vedas call it the Samsara and Santana of existence, which is like a 3D picture show. We are all in the movie or our own karma, and it is this that confines and defines how we act. But there is a DIRECTOR to this performance that we call our life. It is called the CENSOR and it is quite a ruthless creature. In essence, this 'creature' is like a capacitor, it controls and regulates the energy flowing through the ever-present, and ever-changing conditions of our life. It does so to maintain stability.

Much of our religious thought here on Earth is designed specifically to either challenge and defeat, or to win over, the Censor within the individual. As an example: Guilt and Fear are like levers that are put into the thoughts. They are levers used by external forces to direct the energy of the Censor. These things are the norm in most religions.

Such levers, or "strings" serve but one purpose. They are designed to get a person to drop their resistance to external authority. The true purpose, and only lasting value, of Pythagorean Numerology, is to help *remove the reliance on external authority*, and show a person how to become a Master of the own fate.

How Some Paths/Teachings Address the Censor

To communicate with the average person, you must negotiate their internal censor. If you don't, the message will not get through. You can say "this is green!" But if the person wants to see red, then green = red. (There are many ways that a guru or teaching will use to get a person to drop their inner resistance to external influence.) It is all about getting around the dogma, and indoctrination from an early age, which makes a person pre-conditioned to the conformities. These become a "pattern" and it is fine until you want to CHANGE. Then the resistance to change can often be quite incredible.

However, the good news is this. If and when you want to leave your present conditions, find greener grass, etc. there are now many options, faiths and paths to choose that can help. Even so, the Tibetan saying goes: *It is good to be born into a religion, and bad to die in one.* ALL teachings serve a purpose, but you must also outlive this. This book is a teaching in a simple sense. Numerology is a path, but unlike many other paths, I fully expect that you will grow BEYOND the confines of these printed words.

As a practitioner, it is important to understand the religious influence in the Mind of Man. You will find ALL teachings fall into these three categories:

1. **Mind Control,**

2. **Cosmic Consciousness, or**

3. **Movement of Consciousness.**

MIND CONTROL:

This is the most pervasive path in the West today. It ranges from a mother seeking to control her child with will, to the positive mental thinking brigade. One of the more interesting of the modern alternatives of Mind Control is found in a teaching called Scientology. (Personally I do not endorse the techniques, but they do work)

Scientology followed an interesting path in seeking to address the Censor and the associated images that Ron Hubbard called "engrams". That teaching sought to attack the imagery head on and "audit" the individual. With what is similar to the interrogation techniques used by the Catholic Inquisitions, the "audit" challenges and probes every aspect of the psyche, and generally this causes the person to have a religious experience. The opening experience, called "clearing", awakens the Chitta faculty directly, and allows the person to consciously bypass the Censor, and all the rigid social training.

The goal is to get to a state known as "Clear", which is effectively being clear of the conditions that control your thoughts and actions, so that you are the sole arbiter of your own fate. This is done with intense questioning called Auditing. Auditing is a technique to get past the Censor through confrontation, and then literally beating it down.

As I say, I do not endorse the method, which is essentially a mind control technique. Why? Purely because the effect is not lasting. (It does not survive the death of the personality) As a rule, any change that comes about through external sources is temporary. Any change that comes about without generating a COMPLETE integration of Soul and Mind, which means bringing the Censor into line with the genuine and natural purpose of the individual, is a temporary one. It will fade, either in this lifetime, or the next.

COSMIC CONSCIOUSNESS:

Many Buddhist and Charismatic Christian teachings invoke Cosmic Consciousness. This method involves long periods of introspection and devotional behavior, with the goal of awaiting the God Energy (or Spirit) to come and lift you to a high awareness. Many Saints followed this path, which is essentially a passive acceptance of God's Will.

The difficulty is in dealing with the "quiet stuff", the internal mental argument. Followers seek to make everything calm, make it silent. The "monkey's" of your mind are to be corralled. But there is a lack of a driving energy. There is little sense of moving forward in an active way towards a specific goal, and therefore the followers are somewhat passive. This path tends to fall into a state of "quiescence" which is lovely and peaceful, but also a bit of a trap as far as spiritual awakening goes. It is more like having a dream of God without the reality of the moment. Even so a person can achieve spiritual heights. The problem is, what do you DO with it once achieved?

In essence, the individual is awaiting the arrival of the "god stuff" into their being. It does happen, because it is an invitation to Spirit. The problem is, when it does happen, what next? The passive nature engendered by the notion of "God coming into me" tends to create a passive mind that has not trained the imagination.

You EXPERIENCE spiritual forces, but you rarely grasp what is actually happening to you, and thus float like the leaf in the wind. This is the fate of the untrained imagination.

MOVEMENT of CONSCIOUSNESS:

This is where a person lifts their consciousness out of the body, either through natural contemplations techniques or psychedelic drug techniques. The later is not recommended, because once again, there is no training of the imagination involved. An untrained imagination is possibly the greatest threat to harmony and/or finding any sort of stability within.

The most known modern proponents of this technique would be Calos Casteneda. (Recently deceased) He explored both the drug and the natural paths in learning to shift his conscious awareness out from his physical body, gaining a high degree of deep spiritual freedom as a result. He is recommended reading.

Other paths such as the one founded by Paul Twitchell (called Eckankar) offers a fairly complete and tangible set of exercises designed to awaken the students connection with Spirit, and from there allow the student to find their spiritual feet independent of any teaching. The thing is, once you travel past the mind, you KNOW there is more.

The path of Movement of Consciousness is quite defined. Usually a person starts with understanding their dreams, then awakening inside their dream, and finally they start to take charge inside their dream. When the inner consciousness has mastered this, the individual will be able to consciously project their awareness, and in due course, transcend the dream of existence to know only reality at all times.

"Am I a man dreaming I am a butterfly, or a butterfly dreaming I am a man" is the cryptic question core to the Movement of Consciousness path.

DISCOVERING GESTALT

At the end of any path we walk, the principle held by Christian von Ehrenfels is very simple. We are looking for Gestalt, the sense of being whole, complete and unified within.

The Pythagoreans held that we are a song, and that each individual aspect of ourselves is a strand of melody. The goal was to integrate and make harmonious the whole self. I might add that, coming as it did largely from the Orphic Mysteries, the spiritual side of the Pythagoreans were more aligned with the Movement of Consciousness path.

It remains that there are no caves where the rituals of life and death are being practiced now, and we cannot know the hidden side to their teaching. But we can surmise that, as all things Pythagorean revolved around harmony and completion, this was a primary goal. But to achieve ANY of this we need to deal with the Mind and it's aspects.

We must take a very in-depth look at the five main aspects of the mind, the Manas, Censor, Buddhi, Chitta and Ego. As a child these aspects are all cohesive and whole, but in the process of socialization and sexualization they become separate entities within. Mostly, the Censor takes total control, and everything else becomes subservient to it. Gestalt comes when we achieve reintegration of our core elements.

What is important right now is this: When you are talking to someone, be aware that everything you say will be run through their Censor, and stamped "right" or "wrong" so it is very important that we try and gain an insight into what it is, and how to address it.

Focus on the Censor

No matter what path you tread, the Censor will be there every step of the way. It will try and get whatever you are doing, thinking and feeling to conform to the ways and patterns of the present existence. In this arena IT knows how to manipulate and turn your private thoughts and feelings into a way of viewing things that will confirm IT's desire for you. You do not own yourself, in other words.

This creature is really a gestalt of many things: our own inner wishes and drives, out up-bringing, etc. Yet though "manufactured" in a sense, it is a very real thing! It can be inherited from out ancestors as well as grafted onto our being through upbringing and strong experiences. Some call it Satan, some call it Jehovah, but it really is a program running in your mind that approves, likes, dislikes and categorizes your experience. A child does not have a strong Censor, subsequently a child does not have strong likes or dislikes, and a great amount of freedom. Children are very ACCEPTING.

And here is the most basic clue on how best to negotiate your Censor. Acceptance. Be neither for nor against anything, and accept people and situations for what they are. *Be as little children*, as the Bible says.

Each person's individual Censor is built up over a process of years. Slowly it elbows out the natural self and makes your simple, child-like choices seem complicated. At some point, the social training and external influences take over the inner volition of the person, and after that the Censor is running the show. Your Censor is an administrator that is formed from the gestalt of your experience, both in this life and in past lifetimes.

As one example, a brutal Father generally has a brutal censor controlling his actions, and he will pass on this "signature" and impress it into the psyche of his children. The children will then interact with this energy, and incorporate this into their own Aura in a way that "interleaves" the energy of the natural self (Soul - that which is innate and already present) with the external forces being impressed on them.

It is like pressing a key into clay, then taking it away. Behind the impression that is left is an exact replica of the original. Into this mould the stuff of life flows, and takes shape according to the "stamp" that is there. This is what the energy of strong thought and emotion does to consciousness, it "stamps" into it the shape of its belief.

And we ALL have a brutal father of sorts, it is called Society. The shape of our society comes directly from the Catholic-Roman model, and it is this force more than anything that determines the nature of people's Censor.

Western Culture is ruled by the Roman Catholic thought.

The Inquisitions used by the Catholic Church were powerful tools in gaining control of the populace. Fear of consequence lead people to a cowed belief structure, a state of fear, whereby they simply did as they are told. Threaten people with damnation and eternal death, and this tends to encourage a personal worthlessness. This sense of worthlessness, is where the patterns of guilt and control grow. So we build a shield to protect us. We create a way to resist the external forces flooding in.

The minds OWN SURVIVAL MECHANISM creates a "captain", or Director of Affairs, which we call the Censor. It is a defense mechanism against a person self destructing, but it originally grows to defend the child against these external energies.

Thus the weak child gains a hard-nosed, tough "friend" to protect it. If the child wants to run things, it learns that when you are brutal enough and powerful enough, people bow down and accept your rule. So it begins: The Censor grows and the inner child has a parent instilled in their mind. It is a thing that tells them how to behave, and which also defines right or wrong.

Left to their own devices, we find most native cultures have no strong Censor. They have no powerful inner principle that says "NO" to the world. This is what made them such easy targets for control by the more powerfully directed invaders and imperialists.

And what is the first thing imperialists do? They seek to control the minds of the conquered people. They instill a rule of law, and the rule of religion. They create a world of "should". They seek to take on the role of the Censor!

This is a classic case of a Censor consciousness at work. ALL religious authorities, state authorities, in fact any authority, has reserved a 'right of punishment'. They ALL have a censorious attitude to what thoughts and feelings a person "should" have.

There is a benefit to this. People are generally very irresponsible, and focused external authority allows their life to become more ordered, and thus to become productive.

Communicating via the Censor

What we need to simply accept is that when we are dealing with a person, what we are really talking too is their Censor. How someone has been raised, and their present environment will be the platform on which the Censor has been built. But we can negotiate around the current fixed position. Simple questions about someone's childhood, like "Do you remember anything from around age Four?" Will often cause the person to reflect to a time when the Censor was not in control. It can open a door.

We need to remember, most people were trained in fear, guilt and negative threats of punishment as a way to contain the "wild child" within. Fear and guilt are the main weapons used in developing this inner consciousness we call the Censor, but they are by no means the only tools. What I find best to work with are what I call the "gentle" tools. Like a mother educating a child in the best way to behave, we can use kindness, encouragement and praise to shape the message we give.

Inside every fixed, rigid person before you lies a beautiful child wanting to express itself. A perfect example was a woman who came up to me once for Harmonic Therapy. She was like some army major, very strict, very controlled, very dominant. I went through her numbers, and almost everything in her present life was at odds with the Numerical chart. So I constructed a set of harmonics that danced in between all of this.

Six months later, she came to visit me at the property I had in the Northern Rivers of NSW, Australia. Honestly, I did not recognize her, and I said so. She replied "Even my DOG no longer recognizes me!" She was light, happy, breezy, and full of fun. She became what appeared to be the very opposite of the persona she once lived inside.

And this is the point. People live INSIDE a persona, and that persona is controlled by their Censor. But, by using music instead of words, I appealed to a faculty known in the Vedas as CHITTA: The perception of beauty, form and grace. This "perception" ability BYPASSES the Censor. Why? The Censor sees no need to restrict music, or to try and govern it in any way. This is the reason the Church uses bells to call people to prayer. This is also why Rock and Roll was branded the Devil's Music, to try and STOP people becoming too happy and free, thus being no longer controlled by external forces.

The point here is, when we want to communicate with a person, we have to find a way to negotiate the Censor. Otherwise the words will simply be filtered to what IT wants the person to hear. It is not an easy thing to do. Talking with a song-like voice helps.

Here we have to remember an important thing. When we challenge the censor, it fights back. That is its JOB. The censor fights back, and it fights dirty.

This is why we have to be SOOOO careful when speaking with clients about the patterns of their natal charts. Inherent within the chart is the escape clauses that lead someone past their Censor. And the Censor knows it.

I cannot tell you the number of times I have carefully spoken words to gently encourage someone towards a specific course of action, and away from some notion they have asked about, only to have them do exactly the opposite the very next day.

One woman wanted to change her name, and wrote in asking for advice. The chart was clear, and the advice was clear: Do not do it. This is a woman who was already studying Numerology under me, and she wanted a "Stage Name" to practice professionally with. But the name she chose only indicated trouble and conflict. I suggested other options, but I guess they didn't have the "zing" of the name she wanted.

I tried to tell her nicely, but she objected and wanted specific reasons why the name was no good. In the end I said simply "Your choice is purely one of vanity, and I simply cannot endorse your choice." I further pointed out that she has gone through the practitioners course, and why could she not figure this out for herself?

It is not good policy to do this, as a rule. However, this was a person who had passed a practitioner course in Numerology asking the teacher for what was really beginner stuff. She 'should' have known better.

Well, predictably she changed her name to the one she wanted. She wrote back some 2 years later, and what a story it was! The tale she had to tell was one of disaster upon disaster. Someone was trying to kill her, her life was in disarray, she was in poverty. You name it, if something bad could have happened, it happened.

Was she writing to say she had changed her name back to the simple, effective name she had before? No, she wanted advice: if a move to another city would help her situation. Curiously enough, a change was indicated to be fortuitous. In this case I wrote to her suggesting a good time frame to move in order to accent this good fortune.

Her life improved after this. But she never did change her name back to the natural given name that had served her well since she was a child. Standing outside, it was plainly obvious when and why her fortunes changed for the worse. But her Censor was running the show, and that was it. As the old saying goes, nothing so strange as folk.

In many ways, it was my own fault. If I had gone the "stage managed" route, and dressed in black, put on a mask, and acted very mysterious, then I would activate the Chitta faculty in her mind, and bypassed the Censor. This is why the Church uses the all those fancy costumes the priests wear. This is why there is all that gold and ceremony: The flashy show bypasses the Censor. It gets past the natural resistance of the person to external forces with a show that entertains.

You Cannot Defeat the Censor

It was the experience with the name-change woman that helped me focus on how the CENSOR gets in and controls our actions. Something inside her knew, and wanted to sidestep the trouble. Something sent this woman to do the course, and instigated her intuition to write the letter. Something inside her wanted to be free. But the Censor owned her vanity, and in simple terms, it used her vanity to keep her in check.

It cost her everything, her marriage, her income, the health of her child and almost her own life. What is more, until she changes away from the name vanity chose for her, nothing will ever really "hum" for this Soul. Incredibly talented, beautiful and powerful as she was, she was not in charge of her destiny.

But the message to me was perfectly clear: you cannot tell someone something that conflicts with a powerful Censor inside them. The stronger the mind, the stronger the Censor, and until the beams of love open up the heart, the Censor will rule.

In simple terms, we have to learn to dance around this as best as we can. And the fact is, we never fully succeed. Accept this, and you will pull less hair out.

The rule is simple: Until someone gets around their own conditions, you are speaking to a person who is effectively deaf to anything that their Censor does not want to hear.

Rather than fight our Censor, and try and overrule it, it is better, easier and more productive to do something every day that puts us outside of our own mental box. Do something creative, fun, and different every day, and you keep a lifeline to your inner child alive. This also generates a thought field that reaches out to embrace life, rather than pulling in to try and contain it. Simple SERVICE works. A simple attitude of helping others, not criticizing or judging, but doing what we can will break down the hold of our own personal Censor. It creates a sense of OUTFLOW and you feel useful.

When we develop this natural "outflow", we get a certain magnetism, and this speaks more strongly to the client than any words. The best way to convince another to move out of their particular mindset is to give them the feeling of freedom. Everyone wants to be free. To do this you have to be internally free yourself. If YOU, the practitioner, can be free, vital, alive and joyous in your outlook (Well, aim for it at least) then you will activate this "freedom buzz" in your client.

Fun, enthusiasm, a sense of freedom and simple beauty: These are the things that will help another get past their Censor. When someone is in love, the Censor is put to one side, as an example. These are the things that also will get YOU past YOUR censor. The Censor is there to protect you from the outside world. You need to learn to work with it, show it that having YOU in charge is safe, and fun. Then it releases its grip.

Technical Details: Understanding the Censor

The Censor sits in the persona of the individual, and in most circumstances choose what information is passed to the Administration area of the Mind (Buddhi). The Buddhi then passes the Censor's decision to the Ego, (which is what centralizes our internal thought/emotion process) and this is where the ability to ACT lies in the individual.

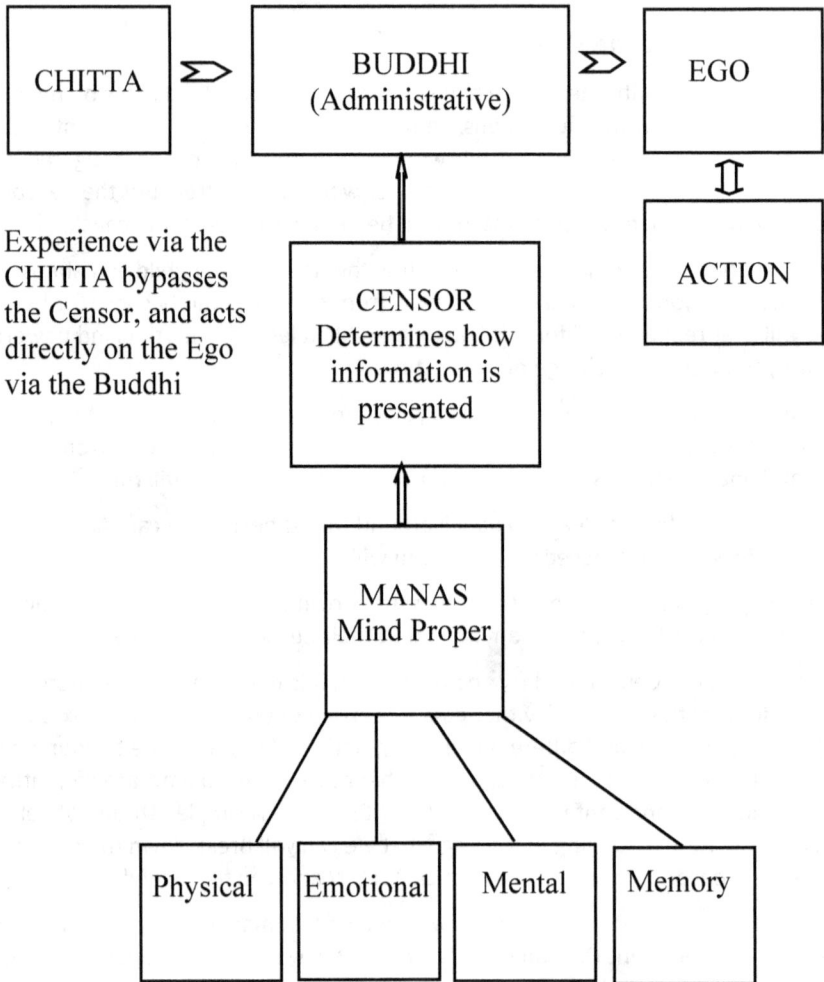

CHITTA ⇨ BUDDHI (Administrative) ⇨ EGO

ACTION ⇕

Experience via the CHITTA bypasses the Censor, and acts directly on the Ego via the Buddhi

CENSOR Determines how information is presented

MANAS Mind Proper

Physical | Emotional | Mental | Memory

External experience channels through one of the internal processes of Body, Emotion, Thought or Memory. The information is passed to the Manas or the area that connects the dots, so to speak.

Book of Number: Client Psychology

The majority of people do not function directly through the Chitta. They do this only when they are in love, or in some situation where doubt is suspended. It's like watching a movie, most plots are totally implausible, but when acted well, and with a good script, people suspend disbelief, and accept it as a sort of reality.

Falling in love is much the same. You simply see no flaws in the person's character, and everything is wonderful. Why? Because your Censor did not get a foot in the door

Beauty and artistic perception is realized within the Chitta. It then passes this perception along to the judging faculty of the Buddhi, or Higher Mind. This hands the judged information down to the EGO, or centralizing unit, which determines Like or Dislike. Normally this process passes from sense experience, through to the Manas, and then it is shaped and formed by the Censor before it passes to the Buddhi.

The Censor sits between the Manas and Buddhi, and colors the image it wants presented to the Ego, or the action station of the mind. So, when you are presented with an experience that seeks to create too much change, the information can be disguised or made to look unattractive in order to get the Ego to register a "Dislike" interpretation.

The Censor uses threads of upbringing, social patterns, concepts of right and wrong, to weave its images. It adds any new interpretation, or energy, onto the cloth of the past, and changes its perception to something less likely to cause change. Why? Because change is something to be avoided. Right at the outset, you developed a Censor specifically to create a safe, known environment, and change threatens this.

The Censor's greatest tool is "comparison". A happy free, experience may threaten its control, so it will take any experience (such as falling in Love) and over time etch into it patterns that will give it back control of the situation. It may be the acid of hurt, or the sense of being a victim that it paints over the "honeymoon", but in some way it will weaken the wonderful sense of being in love, and things come crashing back to Earth.

Now the in-love person starts wondering, "Hey, not good! They chew their nails just like my father". Your Censor uses things that compare the new energy to things from the past. And it does this specifically in ways that diminishes your sense of freedom.

We have the "Chitta" faculty in the mind. This is the area where the person perceives beauty and creativity. This is the doorway your true self. Soul, or whatever you wish to call it, generally uses to try and bring in fresh energy to shake the grip of the Censor. All artists, writers and musicians can ONLY work through the Chitta in order to create, because the Censor is totally devoid of artistic expression.

However, the Censor knows this, and so it conditions what our perceptions of beauty will be. A naked woman can be beautiful, but your Censor will twist the minds natural view, and associate beauty with desire, thus turning beauty into pornography.

In women, it will twist the natural desire for companionship, and make it obsessive or compulsive, so that it becomes a need for unrealistic romance and unfettered attention from a loved one. Or it will make a natural desire to be safe into the need for security.

The Censor seeks to control our natural needs for self-expression and companionship. Animals suffer nothing of this complication, so why do we? Our imagination is why. It is controlled and directed by the Censor, and thus we become slaves to our imaginings.

The Structure of the Mind

The mind has several "departments". There is Manas, or mechanical thought. It's job is to collect the sense impressions and sort them into order. Buddhi is the higher thought, where we find the administrative area of the mind. It also enjoys contemplation and ideals. Buddhi is an internal "judge" of things that are right or wrong for us. The Censor we have been discussing, it is the guardian at the gate, that which stops wild imagination taking charge. The Chitta is the perception of beauty, which absorbs raw expression and hands the images of this to Buddhi, which absorbs and then tags these with a scale of conceptual "rightness" or "wrongness" for the individual.

Like the artist with an ideal to paint, the beauty is perceived, the concept is found right in the Buddhi, then it is passed to the Ego to execute. So the artist dreams, once the dream they have seems "right" they pick up the paint brush, and act.

But if you feel too free, and start being too wild and happy, you may just splash paint around. The Censor will want to step in, and picks up the PAIN brush, and starts trying to control the situation. *It is why so many artists and creative people suffer what is called Bi-Polar, because they are literally being pulled in two directions at once.*

With animals (who have thought processes, despite what some scientists wish to believe) this is a simple procedure. That smells good. It tastes good. I will eat it. If the animal survives better from eating the food, the Manas, or programmable mind area that is like a computer, then accepts that this is OK. No more thought is required. For example: The monkey eats the banana, and doesn't have to think about it.

Yet for the dog, the equation is: Dog food = Yum = EAT. Banana = YUK = LEAVE

In a human, this image goes off to the Manas, where it compared to past experience. The Manas finds: Banana = good. The Censor doesn't argue, and so off it goes to the Buddhi. This looks at the banana-eating pattern, and instructs the Ego. You reach for the banana with a fully programmed set of instructions of what to do with it. Simple.

But we ALSO have imagination, and like the artist, the Chitta faculty can jump in here, and say "Banana Spilt!" An animal cannot do this. Your Manas might say "Diet", but unless your Censor has a pattern to counter this imagination driven desire, the body and the imagination will work together to direct the Buddhi. It is a very complex procedure we now need to follow, and this is where an animal simply does not have the mental structure. We are the ONLY ape to build civilizations, write in a language that is shared, and erect complex forms.

This is because we have imagination!

On a personal level: When desire becomes the driving force, via the Chitta, everything else is cast aside. Here the IMAGINATIVE Faculty is the sixth, and indeed most powerful faculty, within the mind. Your Imagination uses the Chitta to instruct the Buddhi, which pulls up the working patterns from the Manas, after which it instructs the Ego to act. This is not to say the Censor will not fight back. It will make you feel guilty, say you are weak willed, all sorts of stuff to get back in control.

But, in the moment, imagination wins: It is Banana Split Time! This is why it is a spiritual truth that the most dangerous thing for a person is an untrained imagination.

Where We Are Different From Animals - Dog Food Example

The normal process an animal experiences is: An external input triggers the Manas, the Buddhi compares it to past experiences, and chooses to act, run away, whatever

Let's look at a brief example. You open a can of dog food, and you get the smell and go "yuk". But your dog goes "YUM" and the tail starts wagging. Both these reactions are a TRAINED response. Smell goes into Manas, through the Censor to the Buddhi, which determines the reaction you will have, based on past experience.

But if an individual repeatedly beats a dog every time is smells a can of dog food. It will train a different response. The smell of dog food will become associated with pain, and the Buddhi will start a fear response instead of a salivation response. You create a sort of Censor in the dog by training it, either with reward or punishment. It's Pavlov's dog.

Smell itself is UNCONDITIONED until the Censor stamps it with "Yes" or "No". A child may well eat the dog food, because the censor has not yet developed it's "No" stamp. Yet adults almost automatically go "yuck" when presented with dog food on a plate, yes? The Censor has stopped you acting, by conditioning a negative to the smell.

Did you know that the primary choice is selecting a mate with humans comes through our sense of smell? There is some core concept in the back of our minds that either approves a persons smell (pheromones) or otherwise. If we disapprove, and it is not a conscious thought, we will not be able to form a long-lasting relationship with that person.

Yet if someone is RICH, all this will be suspended. The Censor sees money as ultimate security, and it will change our most basic core instincts in order to obtain this. It is true what they say: A person that "smells of money" is attractive.

Animals as a rule do not have this facility. They cannot suspend the natural desires for a higher goal or purpose. Yet we hear about the dog standing beside the dying master, despite it's need for food, and it would certainly appear that the dog has changed it's basic character. I suspect a little of the Chitta faculty can "rub off" in a sense. A dog is truly loved by its master, and it feels a desirable bond beyond its natural conditioning. Perhaps in this way, domestication re-trains the mind of the animals under our care.

We humans are the ones with the imagination to counter our programming, retrain out thoughts, and fall in love. We are the only animal that creates for the sake of creation.

And so, striking the imagination of the client, creating some image or goal that seems entirely desirable, is often a way we can work around their Censor. Simple things like: "I can feel a sense of something greater in you" is often enough to help the client put aside the Censor and actually hear what you have to say. There is a very basic rule of communication: *Imagination is more powerful than facts.* Striking powerful images that appeal to the imagination will often help you communicate far more easily.

I learned this at age 17 when I was out going door to door trying to sell encyclopedia. No one wants to buy an encyclopedia, so I sold them this wonderful write-in service that would answer anything you ever wanted to know. This was pre-internet, and one guy asked me if this "information service" could tell him how to build a space rocket.

Without blinking I said "Of course! Seven volumes thick, with detailed instruction on how to build everything INCLUDING an eighth volume of where to get second hand parts in Russia." I thought he would laugh, because it was SO absurd. No, he said to his wife, "I can build a space rocket!" This is the power of striking the imagination!

SIDE EFFECTS of the CENSOR

Censor action tends to carry an INERTIA, or a "tag", of thought. In much the same way the the Blue Eyed / Brown Eyes experiment where kids became convinced they were superior to each other purely because of the color of their eyes, our Censor becomes convinced of it's place in the world through very limited facts. (Refer: Jane Elliot Wiki)

EXAMPLE ONE: Dog Food not OK for me, but OK for dog = Dog is less than me

Dog is less then me = I am superior = Ego feels good = accepts this postulate. Therefore it is OK to kick the dog if it misbehaves.

This is a Logical Fallacy, but the Blue Eyes / Brown Eyes experiment done many years ago in the States affirms just how easily the Censor will turn internal reality around, and prejudice our beliefs and actions. Your Censor uses Logic in a way that suits itself.

This is why Pythagoras was SO strict in training students in Logical Consistencies. (Refer to Logical Fallacies on the web) This was one way of navigating the Censor. Another way for the mind to process the information about "Smelly Canned Food" is:

EXAMPLE TWO: Can of dog food not OK for me, but dog lovesdog food. I love my Dog = Give my dog lots of dog food. ERGO: Dog eats lots of dog food, Dog loves me, therefore protects the household (Ego feels good, Censor feels safe, world is kept in order)

EXAMPLE THREE: An unconditioned Censor; If a child feeds the dog.

Food for Dog = food?
Food? = taste
Taste = might be interesting

So the Child may well taste the dog food to see what it is like. But if an adult sees this process, they generally interfere saying "That's BAD for you. This is for the dog, and it is dirty." (etc.) The child is effectively chastised or punished for stepping outside the "CEN-SOR FIELD" of the parent. *Thus begins the process where the child begins to take on board the censorious attitudes of the parent*

Get the picture? The patterns of what is acceptable, or otherwise, start infiltrating the mind of the child, and the Censor within it starts to grow.

In essence, the only way around the Censor is to become more accepting of life as it is. (Yet retaining a sense of your own boundaries) Naturally this has its own complications, and the reason for the Censor in the first place is as a survival tool to help the individual not get lost in the ever changing processes of life. So we must become accepting and discriminating all at the same time!

A safe rule of thumb is: Look for the Obvious. Where you find what is obvious you do not need a process of thought, and you are acting clearly and directly. All situations have a self evident truth at heart. If you can't see it, give it time. If after time, it is still not obvious, leave it alone and look for common sense. Common Sense will guide us where nothing else can.

The Spiritual Rule is: Our Level of Awareness = Our level of Acceptance

SUMMARY

Setting a clear objective to become a Master of your OWN destiny is the only thing I can recommend to you.

In the end, it is YOU, the individual, who discovers your own journey. It is a path less traveled, and in fact, you will largely be on your own! No guru, teaching or master can do it for you. We can get assistance along the way, but only the individual can learn how to re-connect with life, and discover their inner path to personal freedom.

The teaching of Pythagorean Numerology, as acknowledged through the Pythagorean Guild, advocates Movement of Consciousness as the path to true and lasting awareness. Indeed, like Neo in "The Matrix" you can move out of your body and EXPERIENCE the "Noumena" or spiritual streams of Number. This allows you to take charge.

When you understand these Number Streams, you will learn to connect with them inwardly. You can hear these streams as Sound and see them as Light, and once you learn to "surf" the light and sound fantastic, you will find yourself taken into the inner worlds. At this point, all answers are yours. When a client asks a question, whatever they need to know will be waiting for you to pass onto them.

You become transparent to the divine impulse.

In this regard, you serve as a vehicle for the divine energy, because as much as you travel out on the Number Flows, they ALSO travel through you, educating your inner being before flowing out to the world around you. It's a very positive, uplifting process for all, when applied correctly.

It is a truly remarkable state, but one that can only be accessed properly when you have learned to negotiate your own mind, and specifically your Censor,

It will takes years for you to learn to deal with your own Censor. There is no rush, and it is always important to keep in mind that the clients you deal with are not interested in anything written in these pages. They just want an answer to a question.

Your job with them is to not just to find the answer to opening the riddle box, but to learn how best to communicate this. If we can't negotiate the traps and pitfalls of our own consciousness how will we move past those within our client?

This is the picture at the end of the tunnel, one of open fields and bright clear sky. There are many miles of experience to walk before we master this ancient art. As always, we start the journey with the first step, and trust that our feet will find the way.

Recommended reading is Susan Blackmore: "The Meme Machine".

This book will show you clear evidence that what you think are "your" thoughts and feelings, are actually hand-me-downs from your society and upbringing.

Next in our study, an area of great importance: LAWS and PRINCIPLES

Laws and Principles

In this section we go over the Laws and Principles behind Pythagorean Numerology. Read them carefully, and allow time for these to settle into your conscious mind. In time understanding will come, but for now, just grasp the notion that there are specific laws and principles at work in any given moment and situation. When you grasp this section, your life will change for the better

Obviously, in these pages we do not expect to fully cover all the Laws and Principles of creation. However, here you will find some new and interesting views on existing principles. I recommend The Theosophical Society for some of their books on the Laws and Principles, in particular "The Seven Rays" as it directly relates to the higher aspects of Numerology.

Also, Paul Twitchell's book from the Late 1960's entitled the "Flute of God" is particularly concise in the area of Spiritual Laws. (IWP Publishing)

There are many interpretations of Spiritual Law, but the fact is the principles are basically common sense and obvious. Pretty much all paths and teachings have their own Spiritual Laws, but precious few of these are described with a basic and functional grasp of how the creative clock of life actually ticks. Many times, the "law" is really a social control measure, such as Sharia Law, the Ten Commandments, etc.

By no means do we go into all of the Spiritual Laws here. This is a general overview of the most relevant ones in the study of Numerology. Yet keep in mind that knowing a Law is very much the same as a lawyer who knows all the facts. It doesn't mean he/she will behave properly. Knowledge is not virtue.

Without principles set firmly in your heart, external information has very little benefit. So as you go through these, try to find a place where the Law or Principle fits in your actual experience, and it will all make more sense.

Again, learning by rote has very little lasting advantage. The whole idea with this book, and this series, is to allow yourself to "soak" up the information, and to grasp what it means by practicing on friends and relatives.

Harmonic Principles and Laws

There are certain, essential aspects to the Harmonic Nature of Life. These Principles are deemed immutable, and can be experienced by any who put in the effort to awaken to the simple truths herein.

The **First** is that **Life is governed by tone**. It can be heard as Sound and it can be seen as Light. This "sound and Light current" occurs on all levels, be it: physical, emotional, mental or spiritual. Religious scripture alludes to this Life Current, and give it many names, such as Spirit, the Breath of God, etc. The Pythagoreans called it the "Music of the Spheres". The Ancient Greeks called it the "E" or the "Ecstasis".

You may have seen an odd point of light floating before you as you went off to sleep, or heard that high pitched tone (that is similar to crickets) at odd moments. Most people will have directly experienced this, but few will have understood what it might be.

The **Second** is that **Life has a natural, though apparently random, harmonic**. This natural flow of energy can be experienced in any forest by just listening to the birds singing, the water tumbling over a waterfall, or by watching the wind blow through the trees. This flow appears random until a Soul reaches a point where they can feel the sensitive energies at play. Then you can begin to recognize the pattern behind all things.

The **Third** is that **Life has Intelligence**. This can be witnessed through the innate patterns that occur that defy the notion of the totally random walk. For example: Such things as Brown Snakes in Australia developing immunity to an introduced poisonous toad within a 50 year period. This is too short a period for natural selection. Then other species of Brown Snake, even though they had no contact with the toad, and lived in different areas, also developed immunity. Such examples appear to defy evolution, but affirm Shelldrake's concepts of Morphic Resonance, or "Intelligent Life Fields".

The **OVERRIDING PRINCIPLE** is: Every Thought, Feeling and Action carries with it, and embodies, a Harmonic Charge.

1. The FIRST PRINCIPLE: **There is a Harmonic Principle governing all of life**. Called the Music of the Spheres by the Pythagoreans, it is often called "Spirit" in our society. "Spirit" is more than some intangible essence. It is intelligent, knowing and completely aware of the moment at all times.

   We can HEAR this Intelligent Harmonic Principle clearly and distinctly when we are attuned to it. We can call it by another ancient name, the Audible Life Stream, for it is similar to a river in that it constantly flowing through our being.

   By tuning in to this Tone Current, our consciousness expands and our natural awareness increases at all levels of our Being.

   Being a part, listening to, or otherwise involving ourselves in this Natural Life Harmony EXPANDS and EMPOWERS the resonance of the natural notes, or Tones, within us, creating greater resonance and energy within the individual.

   This enhances our ability to survive disease and unfortunate circumstance.

An important side note: Life rewards a Harmonic Nature. It creates an expansive energy within us which attracts life-giving sensations, such as love, kindness, affection and good will to all. Conversely, this is decreased or diminished with selfish actions and self-indulgent attitudes.

This is not to say selfish people cannot succeed. We have a Society based on greed. In fact, in such a society, greed IS a harmonic, but it is not an expanding, embracing energy. Instead it is a slowly contracting energy that has a Tonal Quality that invariably leads to an unhappy resonance in old age.

2.   The SECOND PRINCIPLE: **Life has a Natural, Random Harmonic**. All about us there are harmonic fields. These are most obvious in nature, where the natural order of life is most evident. In cities this is more difficult to contact. In populated areas the Harmonic Field is filled with competing energies that tend towards disharmony. Cities are filled with thousands of introduced "hard" radionics from TV, Radio and Cell Phones, as well as AC power grids. It is Harmonic Pollution, and it affects people at a cellular level.

As much as Man pours out harmonic pollution, nature tends to absorb the non-harmonic nature of those who walk within its embrace. Obviously, there is a limit to what the natural order can take before it becomes swamped with the man-made dissonance. But given the room to breath, Natural Life Patterns will flow back where possible.

A striking example is an experiment in the Central North American States where a large area was restored to natural grass lands. All that was done was to fence off an area, then re-introduce some native grasses, and trees. When the natural harmonic of the area began to become restored, creatures long thought extinct in the district mysteriously turned up. Science can give no explanation for this, at least not within its current mind-set.

3.   THE THIRD PRINCIPLE is that **Life is Intelligent**. Life has its own way of determination, but it also has the striking ability to seek to work WITH whatever vehicle is offered to it. Here we need also look at the natural balancing element of Cause and Effect.

Life will support a greedy person, but the very nature of greed, which is to take energy into itself, eventually creates a stagnation of life energy. The result is generally a sense of being trapped. I have yet to meet a person who had negative intention to others, or who was indulgent with what we call the negative emotions, who ALSO experienced a happy old age. One opposes the other.

This may or may not be seen as an aspect of Life intelligence, but it DOES indicate that there is a pattern at work, and that the pattern has structure and adjusts to each individuals situation. By any definition, intelligence is that which can understand a pattern, and yet adapt to a new situation.

This is not a question of "Right V's Wrong", but of frequency and the natural causation. Frequencies that expand and enhance tend to be those determined by society to be "good". Energy that contracts tends to be that which we call "Negative". We could say that both have their place and purpose.

We move up or down the energy frequency according to the inner fineness of thought/feeling, and we expand or contract with the Resonant Harmonic in accordance to the way we move in harmony with life about us.

As an example: Aggression is not necessarily a bad thing, nor is passive behaviour necessarily good. It is more a question of "does this emotion or thought create harmony?" It must be noted that the attitude of goodwill to all is the predominant energy that determines an overall benefit, with the lack thereof creating a detriment, to the Harmonic Focus within the individual.

4. The Overall Principle we are looking at is this: **Every Thought, Feeling and Action carries with it a Harmonic Charge. This "charge" will determine much of how we experience life, and with how life greets us**. (It must be noted the like attracts like, and that opposites also attract.)

The "energy" that is created about each individual comes from many things: Upbringing, genes, karma, past-lives, etc. all speak for the inertia of the past. Choices and options speak for the direction of the future. The gestalt between all these things creates a doorway, the Tibetans call it Mudra, that is the solution to the spiritual, emotional and mental issues a person has in this life.

When aligned, all the positive and negative energies "hum" with a state that allows synchronicity to occur. This is where the miracle of change steps in. This is the point where the individual finds an agreement with the universal.

ALL Tone has a Harmonic Charge. All Tone carries with it a Spectrum of Tone which we can SEE, such as Auric Fields, if we are attuned to this. The Harmonic Charge has therefore an Auric Charge as well. (You can both hear and see the Causal Effect of the Music of the Spheres, in other words.)

Learning to deal with, and recognize, our own energy is the prime focus. Then we are more capable to deal with the various energies thrown about in our environment.

Coming into agreement with the living energies and harmonics within and without of ourselves is the true goal. When we are "in the hum" all things become possible. Ideally, the practitioner will take time to tune into the natural harmonic of their own self every day. Either through singing, contemplation, or some sort of spiritual practice that attunes the heart with the divine.

This may all seem a little bit of a heavy weight thumping of the Numerology Bible, but the core message is exceedingly simple. Forget saving the world, forget the political and social ruminations of how to create a utopian life. Just focus on the harmonic state of being within, and harmony will come around you from without.

Life itself looks after the rest.

Acting upon the Harmonic Principle:

No matter what you do, or where you go, you are interacting with Harmonics. These energies of tone form basic principles that embody life. You are a SONG: Everything you do, think and feel is part of how you are voicing your Song.

We can act upon (and within) this Harmonic Charge most directly though spiritual focus and contemplation. However psychoactive drug use, extreme emotion or fear can also be energetic principles that provide a "filter" through which we can experience a quality of Life. In truth, the sum energy of all things (no matter what it might be) is a "Spectrum of Tone". This song opens up and harmonizes or reacts to the way we interact with it. We might say that everything and anything we do creates doorways, or wormholes, into the pattern of Tone States that is the substance of life. What this means to you and I is simple: Essentially, it is the choices we make that CREATE the paths we walk upon.

In essence, the broader the understanding of any principle that we can hold, the wider and more embracing becomes the Spectrum of Tone we can experience. (Leading to greater awareness and greater experience) It must be noted, however, that temporary shifts made via drug use, emotional or mental gymnastics or any reliance on external input creates what we call "Loop Fields". In other words, unless we go about unfolding in simple and natural ways, we tend to have to go over the same ground again and again. It's a little like the movie "Ground Hog Day"

If we are to realize any significant understanding of the Harmonic Principle at work in our life, we need to shift from our present mind set. This invariably invokes a reaction in the emotions, usually a fear of some sort. Change, while inevitable, is always resisted by the mind. So, as a general principle, in order to realize the truth of Harmonics we must go through the Fear Barrier. This Fear Barrier occurs in varying degrees at all levels of existence. Only when we come to a permanent connection with ourselves as Soul, or Unity do we transcend this frequency of resistance, which is what fear really is.

In this regard, it is important to understand that there are a variety of assorted "Inner" beings (Beings that dwell on planes subtler than the Physical) who live off the vibratory rates of the Harmonic Principle. They are the "Ghosts in the Machine" and exist on all levels of life. Some of these choose to live off the fear generated by Humans, and look to this as their "food". You might note how some dogs enjoy the fear they create when barking at an intruder, as one example. They feed on the fear.

Others beings seek to live off higher emotions, such as altruism. Regardless, there are many entities that literally suck the life energy away from living creatures. These being are the general source of the "vampire tales". I have yet to see a drug addict or alcoholic who is not haunted with a negative creature of this type.

Realizing a full understanding of the Harmonic Principles requires a release from fear on all levels of our being. This also breaks any connection with an entity that may be living off us. Fear itself can be heard as an erratic, dissonant frequency. Unlike the Wild, Natural Energy of Life, which is random yet harmonic sense, (like the chirping of birds in a forest) fear based resonance always carries a sense of impending doom.

FEAR Versus LOVE

A simple rule: *Where fear exists, harmony suffers.* We see this in many ways. The hard boring lines of conventional architecture, the lack of grace in the construction of roads, rigid laws in the courts, and worse, laws that unfairly constrict the individual. Now go to an old town in the Greek Islands, and see the organic architecture, the natural form to the roads, and the easy way that society deals with people. The security of culture in the old Greek towns breed a calmness where fear is not the controlling influence.

Often the straight, angular lines of man-made construction have evolved from a need for order, but they create a stilted, hard energy. Softer curved lines are more harmonic and much better to have in your personal environment. Towns in the Greek Islands conform and grow naturally to their environment, rather than seeking to dominate it.

There are a LOT of control factors in society. One simple word I offer you. Challenge! Challenge the truth of everything and expect to be challenged. You WILL be challenged in your journey to Individuality and Freedom. Because of this reality, it is wise to protect ourselves with Tone Singing of some sort, such as a Mantra. Tone Singing, even singing songs you like, reinforces the Tone Energy within us, and helps us deal with our fears. As a note: Vowel sounds are excellent to use, as they represent the unformed Tonal Currents that our ancestors heard when they were creating language. (A, E, I, O, & U)

You can sing a vowel to yourself when driving along, and slowly you will become aware of a deeper vibration starting to happen in the pit of the stomach. In time, you will enter into the "tone" and feel it all around you.

Of course, the greatest protection comes when we surround ourselves with a sense of love and goodwill to all. This is the most complete Harmonic we can achieve, and of course, like a tree that grows ever higher this creates a never ending process of growth. Essentially, when we hold our being with a sense of love, we feel good, we think better, and we are clearer in every way. We even move more gracefully.

People talk of love versus power: Power is not the opponent of love. Yet it needs to be understood that the desire for power is usually a desire to control. In truth the desire for power is often based on seeking to control the fear based erratic frequencies. There is a place for this, yet we need to be aware that in seeking to control life, we only create greater resistance from life itself, and we are put out of its natural flow.

Power and control over others generally opposes inner truth and harmony. Unless a person is well voiced in personal responsibility and where their boundaries lay, power will corrupt their inner connection with Spirit. Even so, all choices and all experiences lead to greater understanding if our general intention if good.

Harmonic Principles within us LIKE resistance. The more resistance, the greater becomes the life urge of the Soul who in is accord with their true nature. Organizations, such as church groups, will seek to instill a fear 'within' the individual, and try to break this natural resistance. They specifically want to break the inner balance of anyone in their grasp, thus making them more susceptible to external control.

Guilt rules from within, and fear is the face behind its mask. Guilt is a control factor that remains inside the person, and with it implanted in the heart, less use of external force or coercion is required to get that individual to behave in the way another might desire.

GUILT AND CONTROL

Guilt and the conservative tradition are the tools used to control the random, harmonic signatures of freedom in humans. This is not entirely a bad thing, because these random frequencies will empower a person, and without respect for all life they can do much harm to society if not contained. So Control Thinking is imposed by way of the "Should". You "should" do this, etc. You govern society by controlling the wild child within.

Those in power usually seek to control the thoughts and feelings of others through restriction and punishment. A person trapped by controllers can be easily recognized by their inability to express their thoughts and feelings clearly. They literally become myopic (short sighted) and unable to grasp the big picture. Analytical thinking is another tool used to control people, but at least this has a benefit when kept in its place.

Synchronicity, experienced as random events that link happily together, is a clear sign of Harmonic Principles at work in your life. If Synchronicity isn't happening for you, it is a warning sign to reawaken your inner harmonic potentials.

A state of loving-ness towards life (and all things that live) encourages resonance and growth. In place of control thinking, which seeks to discipline our activities with "will", Harmonic Thinking gives a natural discipline that works with the pleasure principles within us. Harmonic Thinking is a far easier way to live. Yes, we still need will power and focus, but these become far more powerful when based in harmony. It all has its place.

Personal Harmony: Liking ourselves, loving ourselves, believing in ourselves. All this is essential to maintaining a harmonic flow within. We need will, but we also need wish, dreaming and fantasy. The essence of the Harmonic Principle is that it is a relaxed state that ALLOWS the natural flow to emerge in any given situation, or moment.

Flights of fancy, out of the body experiences, imagination, spiritual experience: All these are a manifestation of the Harmonic Principles at work. Obviously, it is what we DO with these that counts to the greater or lesser understanding of life. Still, the above represents the energy of a thing called the "Expanding Circle of Harmonic Proportion".

I am talking natural cycles here. Expansion can be a wild growth, like a cancer, or the disciplined natural growth like a tree. We need to invoke the principle of balance and simple common sense in order to maintain the scales of balance within.

Symptoms of depression, circular thinking and fear are all evidence of external efforts at manipulation and the desire to control the Harmonic Force. A depressed person is one struggling to be free of the control levers within their psyche. As a note: All attempts to control the pure and natural energies of Spirit reflect back negatively upon the person seeking to do so. Life will not be controlled, but it can be directed.

This is the secret: *By allowing life to Lead us, we will learn how to lead life.*

When we hold a solid inner balance, we find the natural energies will align and it is far easier to discover our higher purpose. When we allow these energies to play inside our hearts they open doorways to understanding. When we play with life like a musician improvising, playing, being free, we discover freedom. Even so, if there is cold wind blowing inside our house, we will feel the need to protect ourselves from the elemental forces we have stirred, and so we then retract. It is all a balance.

The Samurai of Japan held that harmony was essence. Everything in their training was to create perfect harmony. The perfectly harmonious individual created the perfect harmony in society, and your reputation was defined by the harmony and composure with which you faced life, and death. Dwelling in the moment, experiencing NOW, and serving the higher good were the basic tenants of Samurai society.

Harmony means to be present in the moment, yet most of us hide from this. Most of us cannot be 'face to face', as Saint Paul wrote, with the harmonic process of life. Evidence of this 'hiding' is found in the joining of traditional church groups, and other assorted groups and societies where clear and safe social agreements have been reached.

The general reason we do this is because of the "should" that is really running our thoughts and feelings. The "should" is the core guilt lever used to restrict harmonic freedom and the natural expression of life. How do you remove this? That is the subject of an entire book I wrote, called Ratology: Way of the Un-Dammed. (Amazon.com)

SHADOW CONTROLLER aka THE CENSOR (refer back to: The Censor)

Personal experience creates personal belief. But much of our "experience" is really an osmosis from parents and society, and the way this is defined as personal belief creates "ridge lines" in the auric and resonant fields of the individual. These are largely responsible for the current habits we possess, the patterns which usually control us.

To escape our habits, we generally seek to either remove the "Ego" or alternatively, to use it to enforce our will on the external world. It really doesn't work, and we have a sense of helplessness before the power of our habits and patterns. Yet there is a solution. Allowing greater harmony in our lives is the path that resolves all negative conditions. NB: Challenging the ego, seeking to remove it, or taking any action at all against the ego will only submerge it into a powerful Shadow Controller, and strengthen it.

Shadow Controllers are buried Ego Fragments. They are "tags" or identifiers that live in the subconscious, and manipulate events in our life to feed themselves. Jung calls the collective force of this Shadow Controller the "Censor". (See: The Censor) These energies collate and collect in a mass presumption of right and wrong, and it is these fragments that direct the will of the individual along the lines of prior experience.

These controllers emerge as the "shoulds" that control us. They force us to act in ways that we think we should. Given that common sense usually dictates the best course of action, we would think seeing the obvious in a situation is the best solution. And it is! The Shadow Controller tends to obscure the obvious, and put in its place, beliefs.

These energies dangle on even when the personality of one life is extinguished, and a new incarnation is started. This is the deep and powerful current called the "Ancestral Heritage". We have this pattern in our DNA, in our internal controller, and we also get this inheritance from the actions of our parents and family, our normal external controllers. To understand this process is to understand how the Harmonic "call" draws all things right and proper for our experience to us, even when it appears to be negative.

The Shadow Controller, linked to the belief patterns of the Individual, effectively creates a blinker system. This is a filter that defines all we see along the lines of the belief system that is held to be true. For example: Remember how the Earth used to be flat?

In other words, our bias becomes our reality, rather than just a bias. (Analogy: the Green Spectacles in the Wizard of Oz). As an example: A woman without a veil is seen as obscene by some, yet a woman WITH a veil can be seen as obscene by others.

In other words, our perception of truth and our present beliefs (our unresolved "stuff") create the reality we dwell within. Even before a new and potentially life changing experience arrives, our perceived reality has set up the filter by which it will be seen. Our "reality", therefore, becomes merely a filter. So, what most call "reality" is really a filter over the eyes. It is a conditioning, or coloring, agent over our perception.

Because of this, our reality tends to subtly reinforce itself with itself. We attract people to us who are in agreement with our patterns, and we call wrong those who disagree. Our beliefs generate further beliefs in accord with the procession of images that are our filters of perception and reinforced by the experience that created them. Our programmed illusions are concrete reality until some external force breaks the pattern.

And when change DOES come, life appears to bring pain, but in truth it simply brings new experience. Why? We cannot accept change, and our resistance to change hurts.

Freedom is letting go. Letting go those things which were categorized by the ego and the repressed shadow fragments as "reality" sounds easy, but how do we identify them? THIS is one of the major benefits in Pythagorean Numerology. A good reader can identify these patterns, and lay them out before a person. Believe me, they stand out clearly when you are not in the box of belief that so many are trapped inside.

Again, let us go over the box analogy. The person locked IN the box hears you describe what they are locked in. "It has six flat sides and eight corners" you say, and they say "Yes, tell me something I don't know." Obviously, they can experience exactly what you see on the outside, but this does nothing to change their situation. The difference is that you can walk away, you are free of the box. Our job is to OPEN the lid, SHOW the person the light of reality, and let them see what they have been stuck inside.

Now, much of what you would say to encourage a person to get out of their problems will be rejected by the ego/censor of the client. This is normal. Resistance to change in the norm. So to get around this you use third party stories, anecdotes (or parables if you will) and generally move around the issue affecting the client.

I will use things like: *"I knew a person who came to me with a similar concern, and it turned out that what was really driving the problem was such and such. Can you imagine he never realized that the real cause of this was a deep-seated guilt and fear that he was not good enough?"* This is the third-person technique in the presentation of facts, and it stops the ego arcing up and rejecting things out of hand.

There is always some sort of "stuff" to identify and release in order to create greater room for personal and spiritual freedom. Communicating this takes a far greater skill than spotting it, however.

As an example: At the start of this journey (age 17) I was sitting on the inner planes. A Master came up, pointed towards and open door and green fields, and asked "Are you ready to leave yet?". This simple act is what set me on the journey to truth and enlightenment. This was the first time I realized I was sitting in a box, and that the real journey awaited me. I saw the light, literally. It is waiting for you, as well.

REDEFINING LIFE WITH HARMONICS

This was an inner journey. I came back to physical consciousness and suddenly saw how much guilt and shame from religion had come into me. This is what "put me in the box" and I spent decades resolving these patterns. So always remember, our job is simply to open the lid and let the natural self see reality as it IS, not as they believe it to be.

Thus said, once we shift to a Harmonic Perspective, once we begin to experience the Life Energy DIRECTLY (rather than through shadow controllers and the censor) the energetic principle becomes one of abundance and growth of the new experience. Prior to this, whatever change a person experiences , this is usually just a case of reshaping the new to conform with the old. You can move a moth from the inner city to the seaside, and it will believe everything has changed, but it is still a moth.

How are YOU doing in this area? Are you living outside the square, or are you still controlled by your fears and trapped with false imaginings?

The way to answer this is simply to look at your life, and ask how often you are truly appreciating and living deeply in the present moment. This very moment IS your highest possible reality, and the more you dive into it, the more you will experience this ever greater reality that we call this present moment.

Higher reality can be expressed as the "experience of a broader spectrum of Tone Awareness". This is fascinating, because the pure state of perception (seeing - knowing - being in, and as, a singular gestalt) takes us past the Censor consciousness. When we get to this new ground we come to a world where we are fed with greater and greater states of harmony. The Law is: *Much Gathers More. Less Gathers Loss.*

Which brings us, finally, to an essential Law that governs ALL the Harmonic Principles discussed in this discourse. Contemplate on this, if you will, and see where the thoughts take you.

The Law of Harmonics : *Much Gathers More. Less Gathers Loss.*

It is such a simple thing, but it is a truth that governs all of life. *Much gathers more, less gathers loss.* Another way of saying this is One plus One equals Two, and vice versa.

NOTE: The entire concept of "eating right" "living right" really boils down to creating harmony energy within. By resolving the frequency of mineral, enzyme and the other energetic principles within the body, we can relate these to harmonic signatures and play them back as a recording to assist with internal harmony.

There is currently new technology occurring in health equipment that is working in this field. Decades ago a magnetic resonance listening device known as the "LISTEN" machine was developed, and is one such example. There is also a vibration pattern technology used in the "Orion" machine, and SCENAR tools, which are also very good.

My prediction: Harmonics and resonance are the future of medicine.

RESONANCE

The Principle of Resonance is one of the great, sustaining principles that govern all the universes.

Resonance in its pure form is not subject to Positive or Negative interaction, for it is a State of Being that is called into manifestation only through AGREEMENT. In this, resonance is a pure attribute of Spirit, or Life Itself.

If there is disagreement, or positive/negative interaction of ANY kind that is inharmonious, the pure state of Resonance instantly vanishes.

In its place a secondary energy flows, one that we think of as a resonance, but really it is simply an affinity. In this regard, we have the Law of ATTRACTION coming into play. This is a significantly lesser law to that of Resonance.

The Principle of Resonance is that we, as vehicles of the divine, come to earth as an aspect of God or Divine Energy. In this, we, of our true selves, are in actuality an energy signature that is undivided, or in other words, we are individual.

Further, this "Energy Signature", loosely called "Soul", has a TONE QUALITY, or HUM. We can listen to and call on this "Base Hum", or Harmonic (if we know how) and at any time we can choose to enact a state of complete harmony with our environment.

I might add that if you are successful in doing this, it tends to make very powerful waves outside your environment. It causes reactions from negative forces. A curious thing will happen, and anyone who has a hidden "tag" or ownership issue over you will erupt in a confused way, usually as an assault of some sort, that will be in your general direction.

The only answer to these social consciousness explosions are found in that old propaganda movie about the Atomic Bomb that the US Government put out in the 1950's: Duck and Cover !!!

Resonance is the result of Harmonic Interaction

Resonance, technically, is the vibration that occurs, or is created, when two notes are in harmony. On the wooden sound board of an instrument, the note enters the Sound board, creates a vibration, and this vibration travels up and down the resin lines of the wood. This generates frequency that feeds back to the string and enhances its tone with a multitude of harmonic frequencies. The effect is the single note becomes many.

It then spreads across the wood at right angles, along the fibers of the wood. The interaction of the wave that travels up and down the resin line, and the vibration that moves across the wood creates the RESONANCE of the note you hear.

But it goes further. This RESONANCE also seeks out any note in a harmonic relationship with the played note, and cause that note to sound. In other words, Resonance creates harmony as much as it derives from harmony.

Technically speaking, if I play a note here on Earth, the resonance reaches out to touch every other instrument on the planet. Obviously, the resonant field of just one note is not enough to create a noticeable effect, but the effect is there.

If you, by pure strength of your own beingness, reach inside and discover the pure state of yourself as SOUL, you will vibrate with this and touch everyone in your vicinity. Because everyone IS Soul, they will feel it. They may well react badly to the signal, because after living in darkness a bright light hurts your eyes. But all around you will feel it.

The same goes if you truly touch the deepest level of your vanity. All those around you will feel their own vanity either challenged or stroked. This is how resonance works, a pure note reaches out at touches anything with affinity that is close by.

Resonance is the guiding principle behind the Ken Keyes "Hundredth Monkey" story. One monkey inspires another monkey with a better way to eat food, which inspires another and another. Eventually a critical mass of RESONANCE is reached, and it goes out to teach ALL the monkeys in the area, even those who had no contact with the "educating" monkeys, and they all learn to eat food better.

Of course, in human existence, if you show people a better way to live they usually want to crucify you! As I said: Duck and Cover when spiritual realization hits you.

At a deeper level, we are talking about the natural communication that all things share within Spirit. Again, along the lines of the Principle of Synchronicity, the Principle of Resonance works in accord with how we ALLOW life to participate with us, and equally, how we allow ourselves to participate with life.

Again, resonance requires harmony. If you are feeling out of sorts, not fitting in, not part of the process, you are lacking harmony. Thus what is really happening is that you cannot resonate with your environment.

It is a simple message: We need to evolve a greater resonance within our environment. In this regard, if you wish to create a State of Resonance, there are three choices:

A: Agree with the conditions around you.

B: Change the conditions around you.

C: Leave the area.

Differentiated and Undifferentiated Conditions

We need to take our look at Resonance a step further, and divide existence into the two major groups, Differentiated and Undifferentiated. This is raw truth, and few will understand it on their first reading.

In essence we are talking about a state where a Positive and Negative Polarity exists, and the other, higher state of Singularity. This we loosely term as a place where positive, negative and neutral ALL exist as a singular whole. We could call this Soul, and becoming aware of this is called the Self-Realized State.

Every social group exists as a dual polarity. There is no exception to this rule. Countries, religions, towns, families and individual all tend towards polarity (or duality is another word) and carry an inner tension between the Positive and Negative poles of creation.

These Poles are NOT at the ends of the Earth, they are inside US. The Undifferentiated State is that of the Soul, and while on this planet it needs to find some way to come into an agreement with the condition of Polarity if it is to express any degree of freedom.

There are two basic paths most people take trying to achieve some sort of semblance of this balanced state: *Suppression and Control, or Introspection and Expression*. Neither provide a total answer, but they can be the start of the process by which we discover the undifferentiated self.

Suppression and Control:

The way MOST groups seek to create a "unity" is to seek to suppress variation, thus controlling the Polarity Effect that all groups and individuals generate.

Thus we have dogma, fixed beliefs, adherence to the party line. These are basic tools of censorship, dictatorship and mind control that are so prevalent on Earth.

Most marriages and relationships fall under this category, to one degree or another. This mode generally evokes patriarchal and matriarchal love as the rational behind the need to control, but at heart it is simply a mask for the fear of change.

Introspection and Expression

This is the creative solution, in simple terms. Writers and musicians and poets all tend to pursue this path, and as with all things on Planet Earth, this has its dangers as well.

Mainly creative people get caught up in the Introspection, and allow themselves to be beaten up by the control freaks. If we are too introspective, it immobilizes our survival instinct, and we become a helpless bug for every wandering spider to eat up. Our "worth is unknown even though our height is taken" (nod to Shakespeare) but the external controllers don't care about your internal worth, unless it can be taxed.

Love is the driving force behind the Introspection and Expression Path, and so the person on this path tends to be thrown into the fires of Love again and again, calling it romance for a few lifetimes, looking for the Soul Mate for a few more. Finally they realize it was all just an elaborate avoidance against being controlled by external forces.

Then, at long last, the person discovers a genuine and deep realization of Self-Worth, Self-Sufficiency and Self-Recognition, which leads to a State of GENUINE Freedom.

A little note: When this is about to occur, the 3 - 7 numerical key will be activated. I should also note that this occurs many times in a lifetime before it "clicks" into place.

It's Only Me

In all, the hum, or a State of Resonance, comes about only when a person is able to look in the mirror and realize that they are who they are. When you accept yourself, you also accept you are free, and inner freedom is the cornerstone of true Resonance.

When the Beatles were having arguments, and when it got really heated, John Lennon would look at Paul McCartney over the rim of his glasses, and say "It's OK. It's only me."

This is the key to Resonance. Acceptance! From Resonance flows Harmony and from Harmony flows Agreement (not union) with the Divine.

This Principle of Resonance is both driven by, and drives, the Law of Association. This is the next field of study in the Psychology of the Client.

The Law of Association

The Pickle Principle: Take the worlds best Cucumber, stick it in a jar of pickles, and soon enough it will be a pickle. You may laugh, but this is derived from a book called "The Pickle Principle" and it is a marvelous way to describe the Law of Association.

The above is the simplicity and reality behind the first part of the Law of Association. In summary, the complete Law reads: *We assimilate our environment and in the process we either become it, dominate it, or leave it.*

The variation to this principle comes with the Pendulum Effect of Entrainment. This principle is simply that if you take a room full of pendulums, and start swinging them at random. Come back in 48 hours and you will find EVERY pendulum is swinging in unison with every other one. What is more, test have proven they will be swinging in tune with the LARGEST pendulum in the room.

It is a strange phenomenon called Entrainment, and in a sense it applies to many areas, not just pendulums. In other words, the strongest and most dominant voice in the crowd becomes the voice of the crowd.

Conversely, the weaker voices, as a rule, slowly succumb to the chorus playing around it, until only the drumbeat of the crowd is heard. In the film "Dead Poet's Society" Robyn Williams has children march randomly in a circle, and shows them how easily they fall into step with their brothers. It is a good example how this principle works.

The way to Master the Law of Association is, firstly: to simply choose your associates carefully, and, secondly: always come to any new situation with the principle of choice. You are CHOOSING to agree with what is present, or you seek to alter it, or you leave.

Before you can develop the clear choice to do ANY of this, however, you must already have made the inner choice to be free, not just spiritually, but in as many ways as you can: financially, mentally, emotionally and physically. Only when the choice for freedom is a primary mechanism in your psyche can you hope to master the Law of Association.

May I suggest a simple question to ask yourself with any new Associations you make: "Does this connection enhance or hinder my inner State of Freedom"?

You will be amazed how differently you will start to see the people you meet, and the environment you live in. The next step in understanding this Law comes with learning the art of Focus, and the Art of Patience. These we look at now.

FOCUS

The Principle of FOCUS is essential if anyone is to attain any degree of mastery in any field or endeavor they undertake. True Focus requires a mix of several things.

- First, a degree of CURIOSITY is needed, because the imagination needs to WANT to be part of something if true focus is to come about. Curiosity leads and activates the imagination. Curiosity gives us a reason, or the WHY, to look at something with close focus.

- Second, our ATTENTION will follow our Imagination. This gives us a determination of WHAT we see.

- Third, our base ATTITUDE will shape our Attention, and this determines HOW we see something.

All these three combined give us a sense of WHERE the IT (the thing we are looking at) is positioned in our lives. Herein lies our State of Focus. It is really a state of awareness that starts with, and grows from, a sense of clarity regarding the things around us.

With the above in place, we gain a Focus of Intent, which we project in all that we see. This becomes the tool that operates the inner levers, that open the Inner Doors, that lead us to new discovery, that leads us to FUN.

Discovery is Fun, thus True Focus is designed to activate the Pleasure Principle, which excites the Imagination, which leads our Curiosity, which starts a new cycle of greater Focus. and so on. This becomes what we call the Cycle of Focus.

The graphic below gives the technical details of this cycle. Obviously, the choice at the end of the process is to let it go and move onto the next step, or to create a higher degree of desire. People who get good at focus in a particular area tend to get greedy.

This means they stay in the same cycle of attainment, doing better each time because they know the course, but in the end, it is a wheel. They eventually need to let go and move onto something else.

CYCLE OF FOCUS

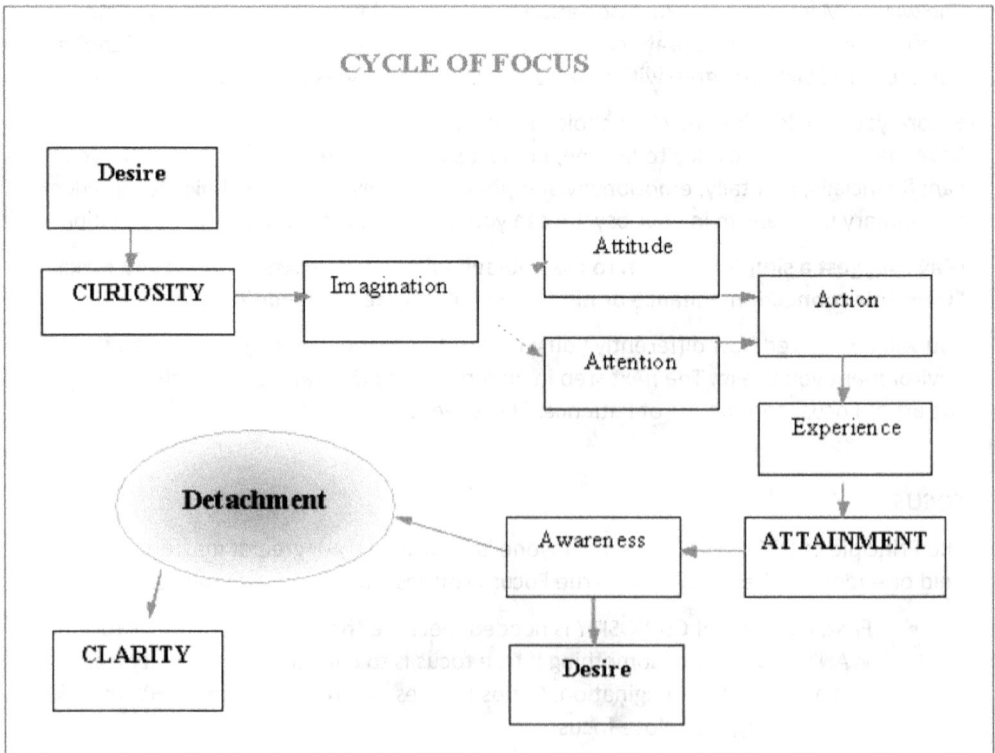

In written form the cycle goes like so:

1. From a Natural Desire, our Curiosity is Piqued.

   This occurs in tandem with awakening or Imagination in this area

2. Curiosity and Imagination combine to activate the Attitude and Attention aspects of the Psyche

3. Depending on the quality of Attention and Attitude, an Action is created.

4. This Action brings Experience

5. Experience brings degrees of Attainment

6. Attainment attracts Awareness

7. Awareness offers a choice between letting go and moving on, or the desire for more of the same.

8. Letting Go brings Greater Clarity and an understanding of our Desire.

9. The Sum Total of this becomes increasing FOCUS and a greater AWARENESS of our present moment.

The End Result of FOCUS, with Clarity and Awareness, is Right Discrimination. We need ever increasing degrees of Detachment to attain increased Right Discrimination. This cycle brings into being a natural flow of Right Action, Right Association and Right Thinking. This results is a Karma-Free Existence.

A very simple exercise to improve our focus is this: Every night as you drop off to sleep, make a mental note of every single thing in your room. Remember it, picture it, take the image of every single item into your thoughts as you go to sleep. Upon awakening, run through a check list, and see how much you remember.

As a clue, it also teaches us the true focus comes most easily when there are less distractions. So MINIMALISE the stuff in your room, and MINIMALIZE your life. Then focus comes far more easily.

So we have our life in order, everything in focus. What now? The PROBLEM with this pretty picture usually comes in the area of ACTION. And the problem here is usually that people act badly, or more specifically, they act at an an inappropriate or misjudged time. As an example: I may fall in love with a girl, and everything is fine, but I ask for her hand in marriage before she is ready, and I blow it. This is one example of unbalanced, poorly timed action.

This brings us to one to the most important principles of this book, and indeed of time itself, the Parable of the Three Moons.

The Three Moons

The Principle of RIGHT ACTION is based in an ancient parable of the Three Moons.

It comes from an ancient source, some say Atlantis. What it represents is CORE to the understanding of Number, and the practice of clarity, right action and freedom.

The First Cycle is one where the Light is weak, and we need patience until Understanding grows.	The Second Cycle is when the Light grows stronger, we begin to see the complete process and start to organize our new growth.	The Third Cycle is when the Light is Full, and we KNOW what out next stage needs to be. This is the place of RIGHT ACTION.

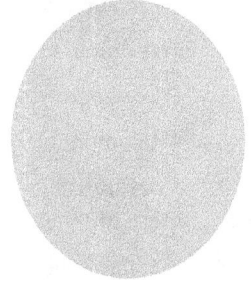

Why do Some Succeed and Most Fail

Most people in this life fail with all they seek to do. This is not because they don't wish to succeed, or don't try to succeed, but mostly because their timing is off. The reason our timing gets off is because we fail to work with the Three Moon principle, and there-fore fail to act rightly, or more to the point, fail to act with strength at the right time.

Let's go through this: The First Moon is when there is No Moon. The sky is dark, and ob-viously this is a bad time to start anything. No decisions should be made because there is no light for understanding your situation. You cannot SEE. If someone seeks to create action in this phase of any project or situation, they will hurt themselves, and others, because they are stumbling into things blindly.

In this phase, the only people who succeed, though only in short bursts, are those who are led by the bonfire of their vanity. The light of vanity shows them a path of sorts. They manage to see a little into the distance, but it is always a short-term success. Yet it seems to those caught in this cycle that vanity and arrogance are the ways to win. Many pursue this path, in some cases for many lifetimes, until they burn themselves out.

The principle to learn in the First Phase of the Moon is PATIENCE

The Second Phase of the Moon:

This emerges when a person learns PATIENCE. It is not bound by TIME, as the actual moon, but by ENERGY. Patience is a trust, a trust in a better outcome, This is what will carry us out of the morass of circumstance, and through the Dark Night of our Soul. This is not a passive state. True Patience is active, and doing all it can to create a better environment, but it does so carefully, and with respect to the present boundaries.

And so, an UNDERSTANDING grows of the situation before us. Our Patience allows an Acceptance, and the Moon Cycle moves on. Every cycle the light grows stronger, and our understanding grows more and more, until the FULL MOON appears and we KNOW. We can see clearly in the midst of night, and we KNOW the right path to take.

So the Second Phase is that of Understanding.

However, some people get caught in the Second Phase of the Moon. They are ALL understanding and compassion, and often in this greater wisdom, they possess a deeper vanity than those caught in the First Phase. It is the trap of the quiescent state, where you feel superior because you remain calm in the face of adversity.

Like the priest who nods his head in silent understanding, but does nothing to help feed the hungry person before him, it can be a strange area of contradiction. It is a place where a person will feel deeply disappointed, and not know why. It is a two pronged energy: One of smug superiority, and the other of a deep need for compassion. It is like the mother hen who will not let her chicks grow up.

This is the Feminine Phase that comes with the second moon, and the Masculine phase that should follow is sabotaged by the need for compassion, rather than action.

The Third Phase of the Moon is the Waxing Moon.

ACTION is the Third Phase. As the Moon passes full bright, the apparent dimming of the light is what causes those in the Second Phase to falter. They have no desire to lose the bright gem they have found, and so they put off the need to act.

This is where the Books of Wisdom become frozen into Dogma and when heroic deeds get locked into Myth. Coming up to the edge of Experience, the person falters, and wonders what will happen should they cut the strings to the past and launch into the future. They have grown comfortable with the quiescent state of apparent balance.

Attachment usually wins, and the person that found understanding tends to distract themselves into a quest for knowledge or they will find and hold a fixed "spiritual" position that will hold some sort of respect for the "illumination" they have found.

The Third Phase is the Action Cycle. The natural process is that, with our the new found understanding of any given situation, we now KNOW what action to take.

Those who step boldly into the new horizon find the path is clear, and the way prepared for them. The past two cycles have been building up and preparing for this moment, and all we have to do is keep our common sense, and much good will come of it.

But rarely is this the case. We may start with the correct action but we tend to get distracted by the myriad of responses that ricochet off the first impulse we put out. It is a negative world, and we need hold fast to our inner truth if we are to survive its whims.

In principle, the path is: Patience grows to Understanding which leads to Right Action.

In practice the path is quite a bit bumpier than this. The natural process is on of lumps and bumps. We tend to have some patience, but lose it, thus delaying understanding. We may get understanding, but our own social upbringing introduced a bias, and we understand wrongly, and so Right Action is hindered.

We may have all good intention, but one little insecurity or guilt may twist something inside, so that we THINK we understand, but really we are just reading a pattern within ourselves. We so often think we are being judicial, but really we are being prejudiced.

It is rarely an easy road for anyone, and if it is, the person tends not to appreciate the destination as much as the person who really worked for it.

The Three Moon principle is old. It is far older than this current civilization, for it is the basic pattern of our shared human existence. The question is, can we understand this process, and then, can we can apply an understanding of this to a client when they ask for a reading? The practice of the Three Moons is very useful in knowing how to "voice" your answers.

How to put the Three Moon Principle to work in your life.

This is the hard part. Book learning is all caught up in the Second Phase, and the real benefit only comes about when we put things into action. Here I am going to suggest something that seems to utterly oppose everything I just wrote.

JUST DO. Don't wait, don't hesitate, do not sit around waiting for wisdom to arise. The truth of the Three Moons is that it is an ACTIVE principle, one that happens as you DO.

You will never become a master analyst of the Pythagorean System unless you practice on people. What happens is this: As you practice, you are starting in a dark, but through your efforts to understand, the light grows. As the understanding grows, you start to KNOW what it right. It is really just that simple.

And it really doesn't matter if you are going in the wrong direction. As long as you are MOVING, you can also change tact, and shift the sails to catch a different breeze. It is when someone is becalmed and passive that nothing can happen.

Get it? The reality of the Three Moon Principles is that it happens INSIDE your actions, INSIDE your heart and INSIDE your mind. Go DO, and everything becomes clear. Just understand that you are doing to grow, and that this inner growth is the driving force.

What I see as a Number Analyst

I rarely see people come to me who are in the First Phase. These people tend to be the "bull at a gate" materialists who are quite headstrong. Yet I do see a LOT of the second phase. Quite often the real reason people have come to see me is because inwardly they know they have to get past a nebulous "New Age Understanding" and get to a greater reality. You get them on your doorstep, talking about a lost love, or similar. Yet what they ask for, or about, is rarely what they actually want.

What most people who call for Number Analysis really want is a pointer in the right direction. They instinctively know they are spinning about in a nowhere zone, and they want direction, so they can find the right action they need to take.

Or they know their direction, but are afraid to take it for whatever reason. Regardless, there is a simple sentence that I recommend that you commit to memory, and say it to yourself in every situation you meet in life.

"Patience brings understanding, which brings the clarity to know what path to take."

The Waking Dream Symbol.

Let me spend a minute to introduce a very powerful, life changing technique.

No matter which phase of their inner moon a person is in, or what their motivation might be, the one hook up that holds them back from just DOING what they need to do is that they often believe they need some sort of a divine clue that "approves" them. They look for an intervention of some higher force to get themselves moving. And the thing is, when you start asking questions of the client, it is usually there, staring them in the face.

But people appear to be unable, or unwilling, to see the obvious. So work with this. You can suggest they choose a symbol or external image that, when it appears, will give them a sense of direction.

When a person is undecided in any course of events, suggest to them that they might seek an Omen, or Waking Dream Symbol. It may be anything, any symbol, but it is best to make it an obtuse one. Get them to choose something that will be a clue to the direction they need. For example: The writing of this course came about when a Raven repeatedly appeared before me, no matter where I was in the world, during 1990.

I put off converting the correspondence course into the book form you currently hold for many years, but one night the Number 53 appeared, and I understood this to mean it was time to start recording all this in the form you currently hold. 53 as a number may well mean nothing to you, but as a Numerologist, the meaning for myself was clear.

One fellow I knew had a difficult relationship, and wondered what direction to take. He asked for a Blue Elephant to appear and that at this point he would see the right advice.

The Blue Elephant appeared on a TV Show, The Simpsons, one night and he got the answer he needed. It took him time, and patience, but finally the understanding came, and with it the knowledge of the right action for himself to take.

It is THAT simple, and that difficult.

This ends the study on Laws and Principles. Next we look at more philosophical concepts, starting with "Knowledge is not Virtue" (Ancient Egyptian saying)

Knowledge is Not Virtue

An Ancient Egyptian Saying went "Knowledge is not Virtue" and here there is much for the Pythagorean Numerologist to understand.

You are being equipped with a vast amount of knowledge in this course. You now hold in your hands thousands of years of condensed information, and you can choose to put this to good use, or otherwise.

Your sense of Virtue will determine what use you put your knowledge to, but quite simply, many people interested in the Mantic Sciences are really not particularly virtuous. In fact, many of them are power hungry egoists. I don't discriminate, or even call this wrong, because life itself will educate anyone who misuses what they have been given.

Naturally, we never consider ourselves in this category. As Emerson once said: *No man ever considered ill of himself, but willingly will see the devil at work with his neighbor.*

The fact remains, there will be many challenges to your virtue in this work. One of the most obvious is the easy adulation you may well receive from people who are looking for a "guru". You can play this role, if you wish, but I have noticed over time that if you do this, you generally discover the well of inspiration drying up inside you.

Another obvious failing is the individual who uses their influence for personal gain, that is gain beyond fair monetary remuneration. The "Personal Gain" can be by way of using others to bolster your own sense of self-respect, or it may be more blatant in that you use this facility to pick up girls/boys, or even friends and acquaintances.

I may do a reading for a friend, but I never do a reading to get a friend.

Your ethics are like the rudder on a ship, and will steer you in the right direction. But more than this, our sense of ethical values gives us a breathing space from the world. They let you step back and listen a little more closely to the natural, inner voice that will always gives us the best direction in the moment.

If, as a reader, you find you are more interested in the pretty eyes of the person in front of you, only one thing is certain: Your focus has become distracted, thus your ability to read the Aspects in the chart will be significantly lessened. The temptation now is to use your knowledge to impress, rather than to serve. This attitude leads to a state of negative inertia, slowly freezing the quality of expression down to a narrow band of insight.

One classical example I discovered was that of the "Egyptian Coffee Cup Reader?

This was a fellow who used to do reading of coffee cups, mostly for middle age women. He had all the lines down perfectly, telling them how they looked, what a nice perfume, etc. The women fluttered their eyes, paid the money, and he gave them a remarkable reading. Now, yes, coffee came out of the Yemen Peninsula in or around the 15th Century, and it became intensely popular in the Arab states. And, yes, there is a history of Turkish coffee cup reading. But what this guy went on with was just incredible.

The apparent and often enormous gullibility of the women who were his clients was something out of a dime store novel. I listened outside the tent, and marveled at the utter inability of his clients to see the obvious.

His patter went along the lines of:

Reader: "I see you have a brother?

Client: " A Sister, actually..."

Reader: "Ah... I thought so... And she is older?"

Client "Younger"

Reader: "Ah yes... I see now... She is perhaps a little jealous?"

Client "I can't see why... She is the pretty one..."

Reader: "Ah yes... But what about the money?"

Client "Well... she is married to a wealthy man...

Reader: "That may well be so ... But what is it that she is jealous about?"

Client "I don't know... Maybe the new car I have?"

Reader: "Perhaps... But maybe it goes deeper... Maybe your Father has influenced this... ?"

Client "Why, yes... I suppose he did spend more time with me..."

This is a true and correct conversation that I overheard. The woman went away saying how the fellow knew she had a sister, and that she had just bought a new car, and that her father had a special connection with her. Unbelievable you say? Well, SHE believed!

This reader knew nothing, got most of his guesses wrong, and ran a predictable line about a parental-sibling rivalry. MOST sisters are jealous of something with their sibling, and MOST people have some sort of parent issue. He was just fishing for facts.

Didn't you love it when he gets the Sibling wrong first up? He guesses a brother. When it turns out to be a sister, he says "Ah! I thought so!"

This is the classic example of no ethics, and no idea other than "I can make money from this". The entire process was fishing, for clients, for information, and for money. Each to their own, but in truth, a wonderful bit of circus, and that is all.

KNOWLEDGE IS NOT VIRTUE

You will not attain any high degree of personal understanding about Numerology when you are giving readings unless there is a degree of virtue being nurtured inside of you.

On the flip side, if you are too restrictive and closed in, with an rigid ethical basis that is really a prison that keeps the real world out, this doesn't work either. This is worse than NO ethics as far as the growth of intuition and inspiration goes.

It's all in the balance. Which is, of course, a virtue!

Patience and Acceptance are the two main pillars on which true Virtue is founded. If we can accept people for what they are and have the patience to deal with the process of life, then we will find the right level of Virtue for ourselves. This is not to say that we accept a thief into our house, but accept them, as a thief, for what they are.

HARMONICS

Einstein was asked about how he came to discover the theory of Relativity. He was asked what the elements were that gave rise to his ground breaking theory. He answered "It occurred to me through intuition, and music was the driving force behind that intuition. My discover was the direct result of musical perception"

This statement should shock the traditionalist in science to their bootstraps, but they really pay it no attention at all. One of the greatest theoretical scientist the world has known, and the CORE to his discovery process is completely ignored? Amazing. The great scientist would sit and play violin, either alone or with other great scientists of his day, and during the course of his playing, ideas and concepts would come to him.

This is a basic lesson in the Principle of Harmonics.

The Universe runs along streams of Harmonic Tones, called by many names by many cultures. The Vedic Scriptures refer to this sound as "Nam" or "Shabda", the Bible calls it "The Word". The Moslem translation calls it "The King of all Sounds".

The Series of Number we use in Numerology is really, at its base, a Harmonic Series. Each Number has a Harmonic Quality, and the interaction of the different numbers has very SPECIFIC and DEFINED relationship to each other. This relationship can be heard.

The Pythagoreans were very focused on the Sound Current. The Music of the Spheres is not some nebulous statement that has survived the millennia, it is a deep insight into the core energy that runs the universe. The electrons in an atom vibrate at MANY TIMES the speed of light. They live in a level of frequency that generates energy, and this energy of itself creates matter, magnetism, gravity, indeed everything.

It is this frequency that exists throughout all matter, time, energy, and space. The entire principle of Numerology is that specific frequencies generate specific realities. The "Noumena" (or unformed energy) coalesces and becomes "Noumenal" and finally it is experienced as phenomena.

Our principle is simple: By analyzing patterns of number, we can isolate and understand each frequency at work within the individual.

This is one of the major developments that I resolved after the initial writing of the original course. The actual practice of converting Number to Music is a little involved, and you would need a deep knowledge of music theory to grasp the intricacies of Modal forms, etc. But this has been done, and if you wish to know more go to the Number Harmonics website. www.numberharmonics.org

Suffice that for the present, Life has a Tone or Harmonic. This Sound you can hear, and many report the first level of this Tone as a high pitched ringing, or buzzing in the ears.

A lot of the time the good doctors tell you it is Tinitus. This is a condition where the hammer and anvil in ear are affected with a crystallization, or a virus, or some other physical cause. This is rare, though doctors as a rule will class ALL cases of "ringing in the ear" in this category.

If you hear an abrasive sound, or a harmonious sound, this reflects your relationship with Spirit at that point. The Sound IS LIFE, itself. It's participation in your life is DIRECT and One to One. This apparently nebulous Tone is your life-force speaking to you.

The Tonal Quality takes on a VOWEL sound, the "A, E, I, O and U" or one of the 12 variations of vowels, In language vowel tones are UNFORMED SOUND. All languages are wrapped around the vowels, which are all the unformed vocal sounds.

Consonants are SHAPED VOWEL TONES, and so the Consonant represents the quality of form. The vocalizing of Sound into Language represents a spiritual dynamic, where the spiritual essence has been brought to Earth, and given form and purpose.

Think about this: The essential difference between higher order and lower order mammals is LANGUAGE. And the source of Language is, in reality, that odd humming or buzzing that you might hear in or around your ears.

This energy is a Celestial Language, spoken before time began, and it is a language which is still heard today. What is more it speaks to you. Right now, it is speaking to you, but generally most people are so wrapped up in the day to day they they cannot hear its gentle, eternal whisper.

If you DO stop and listen, and if you do this for at least 6 months, everything in your life will change. Carefully listen as you go off to sleep, and consciously seek to attune yourself to it, then your spiritual awareness will increase, and life will change dramatically.

A lower quality of the Sound Current is the Light Current, and many times people will experience a Blue or White light like a moon or star before their eyes at odd times. This is the "Light Current" manifesting, and its purpose is simply to light up the path for you on an inner level, to help you find the road home to yourself.

The Sound Current IS the road, however, and is of primary importance when it comes to spiritual growth and deeper understanding.

All the religious texts speak of the Light and Sound, but how many of the priests in their relative religions teach anything about the true spiritual realities? Precious few.

We need to work to attain an understanding of these Spiritual Harmonic Principles. The Spiritual Exercise is like the physical exercise, you need to do it every day in order to build up the strength to attain a higher spiritual pinnacle than where you are now.

If you care to try, I will suggest a basic exercise that has been passed on down through countless millennia: The Light and Sound Exercise.

Quite simply, set aside 20 to 30 minutes every day for this exercise. You must do this every day, for many years, but you will notice a significant result within 6 months if you practice with a genuine heart.

Sit or lie quietly. The main thing is to keep the back straight. (Because the energy that flows through works best that way) and just focus on the Inner Eye (between and just above the eyebrows) or on the Crown Chakra (The point at the top of the head).

- Allow the breath to flow, and sing a word that harmonizes you. It may be "Jesus" or a Christian term, or whatever is right for you. Spirit understands intention. Personally I use the Ancient terms, such as "HU" (Like the name Hugh) or "A-KA-HA" (Ah-Kah-Haa) Both of these terms relate to Spirit.

- Sing your word-song with a long drawn out breath, and do this for 5 to 12 times. Then rest, watch and wait for what unfolds before you. Keep doing this until you feel a sense of being at the "temple within". It is at this point that the light and sound current can contact you most easily.

- When it does, seek to project your self into it, ride with it, flow with it. As you move into the sense of being part of the Current, it will take you out of your body to a place where you will gain an important lesson.

In time, you will be come "strong in the force" and hear and feel the sound current around you at all times. This is when you can start WORKING with this dynamic principle of life. Some simple examples are using this Sound Current as a shield to protect you as you go about your daily business, or holding this Tone up when you feel you are being lied to, or used in some way.

The key element to understand is that you don't have to "do" anything so much as BE YOURSELF. You do not use this current to change things, rather just learn to sit within it, and allow it to move into you, and then it, of itself, will move you to the inner and outer places where you need to be.

If you grasp what is contained within this page, you are on your way to becoming free.

Also, when you learn you can shift your consciousness out and away from your physical body, you will discover a whole new world that opens up for you ... Literally.

Charts become a lot easier to read, as well!

More to the point, you become that beacon of light people are looking for. Our job is to be the fire starter, the spark that lights the inner flame of the client. You cannot be this if your own inner fire is not alive and well.

Numero Ordo Selectorum

This is the Latin Name for the Order of Number.

Number does not 'have" an order, the pattern of Number IS Order. Number is a specific and particular way to describe the known and the unknown universe, and the greatest of our modern mathematicians have only scratched the surface of their meaning. Number and its pattern encompasses the depth and breadth of the natural order.

If Spirit is the breath of God, Number is the voice of Divinity. Number is the way that the Divine Noumena, or unformed essence finds pathways down to manifest into what the Greeks called the Noumenon (Number of itself) and finally to the phenomenal, or physical world. Numbers are considered the bridge between the physical and spiritual.

Pythagoras expressed this concept when he said "All is Number".

He saw the universe from the minutest atom to the greatest Sun as being all derived from, and traveling through, a State of Number. The end consequence of all activity would be: a State of Number.

The movie, The Matrix, was a remarkably lucid way of expressing this ancient truth. Awareness of the Number Value inherent in all things allows Neo (the hero) to master the dark forces and achieve victory,

Obviously, our Western Concept of Number being "one, two, three, four, etc." fails to define in any way the depth to which the Ancients saw the concept. To the Greeks, One represented many things. It was not just a stroke on paper that meant a unit of something, but a whole series of portents and meanings were attached to the concept.

To give you some idea of looking into the obvious to find the obvious: One Bag of potatoes. One cartload of peasants. One unhappy child. These were all derivatives of ONE and in all the above examples the One can determine either One or Many.

But to the Greeks, every number had an almost infinite array of significance. One was primal energy, or source, like the sun. It was Zeus on Mount Olympus, the courage of a person lost in the wilderness. Two move on, and became duality: partnership, internal division, politics, beauty, and so on.

Ancient Greek music was based around improvisation on a simple series of numbers.

Once we understand that the term "ONE" means far more than a unit of something, and "TWO" as two of that thing, we can start to grasp how the Ancient Greeks saw Number. Once we grasp this, we can start **THINKING NUMEROLOGICALLY.**

To this end we now employ time to understand the Harmonic Theology of Number.

In simple terms, these are the principles behind the next leap in reading a person's chart, which is to record their natural harmonics.

Number Describes The Way We Can Heal Ourselves

Number Harmonics has spent over 25 years resolving the basic elements of what Plato described as the Pythagorean System of Healing with Music.

The Three elements that form the bed on which all of the principles and application of the Harmonic Arts rest, are:

- Spirit is Intelligent. It can enter into any temporal condition, and uplift, alter and redirect as it sees fit. However, in all things It follows an evolving sequence of Patterns that evidence themselves as circumstance and synchronicity.

- Spirit works for the Good of the One as well as for the Good of All. It is beyond duality even while It embraces it.

- Spirit works through the divine, eternal aspect of ourselves, that which we know as Soul. As such, we are vehicles for ITS expression.

The Core Element is held that Life (Spirit) follows a Noumenal Pattern of unfolding evolution for the Good of All. This is what we call the Numero Ordo Selectorum.

The method of Pythagorean Tone Healing relies on simple principles:

- **The Music of the Spheres**: All around us there is a Tonal Bath of Sound and Light, which the Pythagoreans called the Music of the Spheres. This is what we call "Spirit" in the West. This Tone Current, or Audible Life Stream, alters from one day to the next, and from one moment to the next, in a specific pattern of unfolding and refolding tones.

- **All is Number:** In the process of Life, the patterns of Number represent the Patterns of Divine Order. These Patterns, once understood, can be described Harmonically. This is Mathematics as Music.

- **Each Date is a Harmonic Map:** The simple "map" of these Number Cycles is found inherent in the date of every day. A Date is really a logical dialing up of repeating cycles, always with an element of "one" added from the prior date.

- **Each Individual Has an Overall Harmonic Map: You are a Song.** By looking at the Important Dates in a person's life, we can see what specific Divine Energies are being called in on those days. Thus we can plot out a specific "Unified Tone Map" for each individual.

An overriding principle in all Pythagorean thought is that **"There is no coincidence"**.

Tone Healing applies equally to Mental, Emotional and Physical conditions, and can also greatly assist opening up of spiritual understanding in people.

It should be noted that people need not believe in this system for it to be effective. It works regardless of the belief or non-belief by the Listener. In fact, Non-Belief often is more effective, because when the changes become overt, the person is so surprised that they tend to become very involved in their process. In the end, it is the personal energy we put in towards unfoldment that counts.

On a personal level, the Pythagoreans held the Following:

- We are Soul. Soul is an eternal Spark that cannot be extinguished, inverted, or harmed.

- Soul travels from incarnation to incarnation perfecting its understanding of Its Spiritual Purpose.

- Soul has no Gender, and is not subject to Polarity of any kind

- Soul, once awakened, lives consciously in the High Worlds of Spirit

- Soul knows only Harmony.

Subsequent to this, if someone is struggling under a burden of dis-ease or suffering deep anger or emotional/mental anguish, this is simply an indication that the individual has lost, for that period, the direct connection with themselves as Soul. This is not to say that a person who gets ill is no longer spiritual, aswe all go through cycles, but when the focus in on the spiritual, you do feel it less.

By "retuning" people to their "Soul Patterns" (that which is mathematically inherent in the important dates of their life) an individual begins to naturally flow back to a point of "Soul Harmony" rather than one of Mental or Emotional conflict. **It MUST be noted**, however, that with the journey back to that state of harmony, the individual often goes through significant conflict. We work for everything we get.

An over riding principle that governs all of life is that, as Soul, we make agreements. We call the result of these agreements "Karma" or "Fate" or just "Gods Will", but these are just names. Our "agreements" are evidenced by the events of our lives, and there is nothing left purely to chance. So the date of an important event reflects the agreement.

Despite any contrary belief, the Pythagorean Analyst will see your agreements reflected in the dates of certain events. The Patterns are definite, and there is no happenstance or guesswork involved.

If you are interested in having your Tone Chart worked out for you: Please go to the Number Harmonics web site. www.numberharmonics.org

NOTE: The Core of Ancient Greek Philosophy revolved around the contrary argument of the Hedonist Versus the Idealist. Should I enjoy the moment, or prepare for the future? Should I indulge my appetite, or watch my weight? All the contrary questions that run through us ran through the Ancient Greek civilization as well.

This is why the Greeks worshipped Music as the highest of the arts, because in listening to exquisite music there was no longer an argument within a person. Both aspects of our being could equally enjoy the moment. The core of this is simple: Quality Music naturally instills a sense of Higher Consciousness. Higher Consciousness answers all the questions of Human Existence.

This remains a basic principle and guiding light with the application of the Pythagorean Art of Toning for spiritual, mental, emotional and physical well-being.

VASES at the PORTAL

Illustration: David Kemp

There are Two Vases at the Portal of our Conscious Awareness. One is full of our deepest Dreams, Wishes and Unexpressed Feelings. The other contains all the hurt, disappointments and whispers within. Every day, with each moment, and often unknowingly, we sip a dram from one of these Vases. Every moment of every day we dip our cup in one, and sip on the dreams or the whispers we extract.

These small choices from within our deepest being create everything we experience. The dreams and whispers we sup upon arrive as secret, silent advice on how to act or behave in any given moment. What we receive from either vase determines how we will act and feel for the next cycle. And usually the message is Bitter-Sweet.

In both Vases, the messages are not so much written on paper as distilled as a sweet or sour wine. Each drop of this wine carries the flavor of a thousand secret promises or poisons. One Vase contains the bitter: bitter to taste, yet like coffee it can be addictive. The other holds the sweet. It is often too sweet and unrealistic for the reasoning mind, and yet we find we have a sweet tooth that desperately needs this nectar.

The Bitter Vase is marked "Whispers" while the Sweet is marked "Aspirations". And each day the secret question we ask ourselves is this: *Do I choose to take from the Vase of Whispers, or from the Vase of Aspiration?*

The Vase of Whispers contains all the hidden secrets of our fears. It is full of the sum total of our failures, and all the messages of those who have told we are no good. Here are all the combined dramas and broken dreams that have caused us to develop the fears we hold dear. This Vase hides the dark angry places inside us.

The Vase of Aspiration holds the loving memories. The dog we played with, the warm hugs from our mother, and the simple joy of being. Every piece of positive reinforcement and joyful experience we have ever had is a drop of Aspiration, condensed to an expectation of success, love and happiness.

The Vase of Whispers contains the sum total of our thoughts of control and domination over others, and it is the place we go when we believe we are in opposition to the world about us. Your Whispers will always encourage you to TAKE and DOMINATE.

The Vase of Inspiration is where we have stored all our finest thoughts. The hopes, dreams and wishes for a greater future which we put there (or were placed there) in our childhood. This is where Superman is you, and the hero always wins. It holds messages that tell us how we can grow and develop, and become truly great.

This place of inspiration always *seeks to make ourselves and the world a better place.* Your Inspiration always encourages you to GIVE and SERVE

When we feel free and independent within ourselves, we are supping from the Vase of Inspiration. When we are insecure, and needing, we are supping from the Vase of Whispers.

Every day, in a thousand ways, we choose which Vase we will draw from. The smiling little girl causes us to draw from our aspirations, the sour bank manage impels us to draw from our whispers. The triggers are everywhere. Do we need the Sour Taste of Hard Experience or the Sweet Aroma of Dreams?

And on top of the choices, we are two faced. One face looks outward at society, one face stares blankly within. Perhaps: A passive, kind person without, a hungry panther within. Or the aggressive strong man to the world, a scared rabbit within. So many people locked in an inner argument that keeps them from natural harmony and freedom.

Feeling pity will not help. That is arrogance. What is needed is to grow past the Two, and find the creative Three inside us. Unite our inner and outer selves by choosing to make a better self, every day. The simple truth is that we need BOTH Vases, and our two faced nature, if we are to survive in this world. They are BOTH a gift, and it is how we USE these gifts that either help or hinder our spiritual and emotional growth.

The answer is found when we learn to match the sweet with the sour, the high with the low, the small with the grand. These Vases represent the polarities within our own being. We have in our hearts a map that guides the left hand to the darkness, and the right to the light. Or it may be vice versa for you. What is of importance is that because of the polarity within, the CHOICE is there to take a new direction, every moment.

Our CHOICE has usually been cast like dice at an early age. We have seen the number of our fate written by parents and society, and we are playing out it's chance. We are choosing through REFLEX to sup on the negatives or positive in any given situation. And until we have a change of heart, or a breaking through to a greater love, we will simply follow the set course, one that the inertia of our upbringing chooses for us.

The question remains: What are you CHOOSING right now? Choice is a CORE FUNCTION of the persona. For example: Are we first listening and then deciding to act, or have we decided, then maybe thought about listening? Think about this in particular, if you will. Most decide their path with their secret prejudice, then pretend to listen.

The basic choice most make is to not choose, and just follow a set pattern. Yet humans can rise above instinct, we can change the program. The instinctive, or programmed, choice is what tells our hand to select from the Vase of Whispers, or the Vase of Aspirations. But if we choose to be aware, we can change this pattern.

It's a Matter of Balance

Everyone has a Positive and a Negative potential, and depending on the nature of our being, we draw a little from both aspects. When we discover inner balance, the Neutral State, we learn to redefine our choices, and take what we need from each moment in order to match the situation we face. We "de-side": We start choosing the pure state of BEING over the eternally alternating positive / negative states within us.

As we find balance inside ourselves, we learn to resolve and COMPLETE each moment in our outer world. How do we complete a moment? Just look at any young child, and re-learn the art of immersion. If you can just live in your moment completely, you will soon re-discover what it is like to complete your given point of NOW.

In time, we all will learn to draw from each moment what we need, like it is a well. We learn to create the future we truly know and understand to be the best for all. How well we do this is based on both where we place our **Attention** and how pure our **Intention** is. These two things, of themselves, are the cornerstones of our truest belief and faith.

Before this, we dip the cup of our present awareness a little into both Vases, mixing them up and seeking to find the right balance with which we can deal with our environment. But we tend to do so unknowingly. Freedom means we must do so knowingly.

Fact One: The hand compulsively reaches for the Vase that our habits have trained us to reach for. Like any habit, it must be broken before we can rise above it.

Know this: In this process of "habit breaking" we will discover there are deeper secrets in our hearts, and that a good deal of the thoughts we believed were our own are really "Hand-Me-Down" notions from parents and society. These "Hand-Me-Downs" or MEMES form a collective resistance pattern to change, one that reinforces the CENSOR.

We need to get past our Censor and our habits to find the natural path that leads us to an increase in freedom and harmony.

The Study of Truth, wherever you may find it, and whatever it is to you, is one way to help break the "reflex" habits we have collected in our upbringing. As we go through this process of self-growth and inner understanding, we will find, more and more, that we are moving into a position of INNER CHOICE with how we deal with the NOW, which then helps us deal with all our external situations.

Fact Two: In the end, we must learn to master ourselves to the degree where we CHOOSE our action or reaction to any given moment. At this time, we learn to choose not so much from our fearful Whispers or confident Aspirations, but from the well of our true, inner being. Only then do we know true freedom.

In time, we go past ALL of that which is the past within us. We break the back of the karma that has entrained us to act like the mouse on a wheel, and finally we establish a **fountain of new awareness within ourselves**. This is the only true Initiation. Only then in this "reborn" state do all the aspects of the past, and the potential futures, become less important to us than the process of our present moment.

For the Spiritual Student, this "fountain" comes as an awareness of a never ending stream of Light and Sound. This is the Fountain of Youth: An ever present flow of Tone and Inner Truth that gives a clear message of the way to go in every moment of every day. What is more, it is already there, inside your heart. You just have to rediscover it.

How do we re-discover this eternal stream of life? We need but take the time to listen to life, and decide to be a part of it. Sadly, most don't listen, and are never really a part of the life that is all about them.

Pythagoras taught that we must listen to the Inner Music, the Music of the Spheres, and to do this every day. This is the fountain of youth. He taught that we must discipline the mind with silence, in order to hear the natural flow of Spirit. The perfected man trained the mind with science, and the heart with music.

We all have an Inner song that our heart wants to sing. We need to tune into it, to listen to its aspirations AND its whispers. This gives the heart wisdom the Egyptians prized, this gives the Omphalos, the point where you become the center of all truth.

This then is the simple secret: The heart whispers with the soft voice of a lover, and its aspirations are always kind. Keep the simple spiritual discipline of just listening for the Music Of the Spheres, and looking for the Light of Understanding. Spend time each day, stopping the mind, and looking within to find this harmony. With patience we will grow past the confines of our past, and arrive at the reality of our present.

Fact Three: We must EXERCISE our right to choose by choosing. How best to do this?

The simple message of this narrative is this: Spend 20 to 30 minutes every day in contemplation. Look for the Light, which can come as a Blue of White star or moon, and listen for the sound, which often comes as a high pitched tone in or around our ears.

The choice to do this leads to freedom. In a short space of time, you may find yourself drawn deeply into this simple gift of the Divinities. If this is so, you will find your conscious awareness lifted out of the physical body, and you will (in the words of Socrates) "Be lifted unto the aethers, whereupon thyself shall be as a God"

You, as Soul, are the mirror of Divinity. Your choice is simple: either polish and clarify, or live in fear and distort, the reflection you find therein. Your job is, like Alice, to fall through the looking glass and make sense of the new world you encounter.

Right now you are at the doorway. This is the place which IS the new horizon, the new experience, the greater state of BEING. Walk through this very moment, and you will find yourself waiting for you, Explore whatever is here RIGHT NOW and you discover self. When you do this, the new paths, the new choices will open to you. Like a flower opening to the sun, so too will your heart open to the new day as it dawns.

How do we allow in the Sun, how do we find this new dawn? By letting go of our hold on our dark night, where all the whispers and fears come to haunt us. Then slowly, naturally, our mind will transfer our trust to the Vase of Aspiration, yet at the same time, pay heed to the doubts and warnings of our Whispers. We need them both. Fulfillment and Aspiration are waiting for you to drink your fill, but without the Whispers, you will too soon be drunk upon your own divinity, and fall like Iccarus.

And through it all, through all the dark nights, the lonely afternoons, the ups and downs, through all the clouds and rain and sunshine, the letter from the divine that has our name on it will always arrive on our doorstep as a paradox.

The paradox is ever this: Without the night, we cannot recognize the day. Until the Day is Night and the Night is Day, we know nothing of either, and we will remain chained to the skeletons of the past.

This ends "Client Psychology". Please consider over the next few years a little of the concepts written into these words, and as there truth awakens in you, the depth and knowledge of the ancients will become manifest in your life.

However, let it be clearly known that no Soul can hope to encompass all of knowledge or wisdom. What we have recorded here are the "Bones of Truth". It is the core material that is pivotal to Pythagorean Numerology. You journey will be different and unique. Yet no matter where you go and what you discover, you will find again and again the same truths that we outline here.

Life is a mirror, and our face reflects the universal being.

The question that remains is a very old one: *What side of the mirror are we on?*

Are you ready for the next step?

From the same writer, we bring you the Divinity Dice Series.

DIVINITY DICE

Play the Dice of the Gods

Cast the Dice of the Gods and allow Life to give you
the answers to your deepest, most secret questions

*Insta-idea-vit:
(Let the Dice Fly High!)
Julius Caesar*

Author: Michael Wallace

Play the Game of Life
Have Fun with Divinity Dice and discover amazing
answers to your deepest questions. Discover how the
Ancient Art of Prophecy is still alive in the 21st Century.
The Greatest Secret is in Your Hands Right Now!

Divinity Dice is produced under the authority
and auspices of the Pythagorean Guild.

These books were written to help a Numerology Student grasp how number combinations worked. They provide an easy, practical way to give a natural numerical reading, based on the various castings of the polyhedral dice.

Go to divinitydice.com.au for more information and current pricing.

There are also a series of workshops available, which allows the Numerologist to communicate the power of number to the general public.

Without doubt, the most comprehensive books on Dice Divination on the planet.
George Cockcroft, writer of "The Diceman"

The PURPLE PLASMA BALL

In closing this work on Client Psychology, I would like to end with an experience I was given as I finished writing this book. You could call it a Spiritual experience, but really, it is how Life talks to those who listen. Life works like this, we dedicate ourselves to a specific purpose, and it comes along behind us, and fills in the blanks.

Yesterday, I closed my eyes, very tired from the work involved with compiling all this information, and immediately I fell into a very deep state. My little cat leapt up onto the bed as I dropped off, and then I was in another place, another time.

A battle was raging, and in this a pure, purple plasma ball was floating. I watched it, and realised the ball was a being. Then "I" was that Purple Plasma, gazing out with a 360 degree view. A friend calls out, and says "Be a gun, and keep the enemy away"

I am a little confused, but I imagine I am a gun, and as soon as I imagine this clearly, this is what I am: A gun pointing at the enemy, warning them to stay away. But the enemy is not easily shaken, and they make threats. Their cruelty triggers off a powerful response, and any sense of holding back vanishes. My mind opens up and I blast their weapons, clothes, and even their dignity, from them, pinning them to the ground through sheer force of will. I realise I am power, itself, and whatever I imagine will come to pass.

I felt this pure, pulsing energy running through every atom, and I KNEW, I knew my thoughts and feelings would come to pass. As I come back to physical consciousness, I realise the last section of this book must be about the IMAGINATION. I see that the experience was simply to make me aware that this is the primary power within us all, the power of imagination.

And it comes to me to ask you, what IS imagination?

Charlie "Bird" Parker, the famed sax player, was once asked if he was happy with where he was at in his playing. He said, quietly and thoughtfully, "Yeah, I am. All I have to do is IMAGINE what I want to play, and my fingers are already doing it."

People tend to think imagination is a fragile child-like dream. And for most, their untrained imaginations are just this: Child-like and impotent. But when you marry your imagination to a directed will, everything changes. There is no force as strong, no power greater, than that of the focused imagination directed by our true nature.

I was given the clue of a purple plasma ball purely so I would remember the experience, but at the same time, the universe runs on plasma. So Spirit is also being a little cute, because it knows the universe did not manifest from a "big bang" but emerges from and continues to be energised, by plasma interacting with the natural forces. (Read: The Electric Universe by Wallace Thornhill & David Talbott)

99.99 % of everything, including so-called empty space is plasma. But for creation to form, this plasma has to be focused, organised, and coalesced into form. Our entire creation is really a spark of divine imagination acting on the plasma of life itself. And just as Divinity can create, so too can we, the children of divinity, create.

How? By using focused, clear imagination. As an example: If you wish to be a good reader, study the work provided, learn the interpretations, and be dedicated to helping others. You will do well, but if you have no imagination, if you cannot see within yourself how the various Aspects knit together and form a unique whole, then you are basically a mechanic taking things apart and putting them back together again.

The message: *Without imagination, we are mechanical beings.*

As a Purple Plasma Ball, it took time for me to realise my own power. I was fettered and held back by the belief of being ordinary, but when I let go on my smallness, I realised that inside the heart is a power beyond measure. All we need do is imagine, believe and act without doubt or compromise, and the world will form into the shape of our dream, and it will become reality. Ideally, it manifests for the good of all.

The journey to truth is really the journey to making dreams a reality. The child starts this life with nothing but it's enthusiasm and imagination. It has no money, no clothes, no trappings of any sort, but what it carries is the power to dream. It has the power to learn, to grow and to imagine, and in due course, to turn all of this into a new reality.

Our imagination is really the thought of true self flowing through into our mind. If you could separate yourself from your thoughts, you would experience this power first hand. Your clients have this power inside them, but it needs to be encouraged. And if you do not trust your own imagination, if you cannot pick up on the subtle clues that Souls thought is giving you, then how you can expect them to?

Your job, should you choose to accept it, is to learn to trust, develop and discipline your own imagination. It is everything in this work.

I had to imagine writing this book before it could be written. I had to imagine writing the correspondence course before I could run classes in Numerology. We all must imagine our way to a greater future before we can hope to claim it, because our imagination is way we find the road to truth.

Einstein wrote his theories only because he IMAGINED they could to true before he started. Everything and everyone is tested, but this simply refines the imagination, and with focus, effort and heartfelt intent, we cross all barriers and reach the natural state, where beingness and truth become self-evident.

You will know when you have achieved mastery of this work when you can look at a chart, see the pattern of numbers before you, and in your imagination the answer is laid out before you. You will discover that reading a chart is no more difficult than reading a book, and that all you are really interested in is reading interesting books. Everyone will become, for you, a Book of Number.

For now, the journey is simply to discover how this all adds up!

INITIATION

A final note. You can be the worlds greatest Numerologist, you might understand the deepest significance of every Aspect and permutation in a chart, and have the closest connection to the inner workings of the Spiritual forces: But if you don't DO anything with it, you are useless.

We think of Initiation as some external right of approval, and on one level it is. Yet unless you DO, no one can recognize your ability, yes? the simple fact is that all the study and learning will not make you a Numerologist, only DOING creates achievement.

This said, there is still an inner Initiation into the Pythagorean teaching. It is a very real thing, despite the 2400 years that have passed since it was first inaugurated. There have been quite a few called to the original course who were students from the ancient times, coming as it were to refresh the connection.

As I started recording all of this information in 1991, I was visited by Pythagoras. I was ushered into a vast, empty hall that was the main teaching temple in his day. The thing I noted was the sheer emptiness, no one was there but we two. In my mind, the question was very simple: Is it my job to fill the hall? There was no specific answer. Was it best to let sleeping dogs lie, and let the past remain the past? Or did I forge on, knowing as I did that the task of re-creating the Pythagorean teaching was a long, hard road.

When I came back to the physical, my only notion was: It's something I want to do. So I continued writing the original course, and the doors to understanding (that which is the true initiation) kept opening for me. Many things shifted in my outer world, but the inner task remained. Yet I didn't ever think of it as a task. It was simply what I was did.

And as things panned out, raising my youngest on a secluded property, where I needed to be on hand, meant that I had many hours every day to work on the Pythagorean principles. I resolved the secret to harmonic healing, and put up the Number Harmonics website in 2000. When the secrets of Harmonics were mastered, I worked on resolving how the Pythagoreans used polyhedral dice to teach math patterns and divination to students. This study was the core to the Divinity Dice series of books.

And all of this evolved out of the original study course, by just DOING. Finally it comes full circle and this course is to be made open for general public study. All of this came without any "outer stamp" of approval, or anything other than the many thousands of clients who continually told me it seemed miraculous, etc.

Then it finally dawns on me: Initiation! This is simply taking the INITIATIVE, this is the act of DOING, that brings into BEING the truth. Every step along the way, every door that opened, was an initiation into a new state. Finally, friends who had followed this process for over 35 year declared to me it had been achieved, the ancient path had been woken so that others may tread it should they choose.

Should you wish to become recognised as a teacher or practitioner of this art, there is a process of qualification in place now. But in truth, it is what you DO that matters.

www.bookofnumber.com.au

For further enquiries and updates go to the official web page at bookofnumber.com.au. There you will find all current information on Pythagorean Numerology, as well as where you can find study groups, on line classes and areas of interest to the subject.

Michael Wallace (Raven)

Michael Wallace is a remarkable individual. He is a Master Musician, Master Body Worker, Master Numerologist, Dice Master, Recording Artist, Songwriter, and Publisher. On top of all this he is also a prolific writer with over 17 titles in print.

Known as "Raven", or what the Hopi describe as the Storm Bringer, he is a catalyst for change and renewal.

www.numberharmonics.org

The original site for the Pythagorean system of Harmonic Healing.

www.divinitydice.com.au

The main site for the study of Dice Divination, based on the Pythagorean Polyhedral Dice

Enquiries should be made to the publishers at this Email Address.
Info.numberharmonics@gmail.com

ISBN: 978-0-9756994-5-4
Copyright 2014 Michael Wallace